REVIEWS

'It will transform your ideas of dull daily Bible reading into opp___ ___ities for daring daily Bible doing. The creativity, energy and fresh challenge of each reading fizzes on the page.'
Christianity magazine

'This compact volume of devotions by YFC worship leader Andy Flannagan is like no other I've dipped into. It's ultra-relevant, up-to-date and spiritually challenging – with its practical meditations, prayers and life-steps rooted in the Bible. Andy's applications of God's timeless words find their context in our interaction with neighbours, our friends and family and our approach to the typical daily challenges of life. Fantastic stuff!'
Deanna Fletcher, DJ, Revolution Radio, Direction magazine

'Andy Flannagan turns the whole quiet time thing on its head. Providing 120 devotionals that not only get you into the Bible but also get you out doing things in the world, this book could just revolutionise the way you live out your faith.'
Inspire magazine

'This readable book gives us a set of guidelines which challenge our "normal" approach to thought and prayer, which asks the questions that some of us are afraid to answer, but which is refreshing and candid in its method. 120 experiential devotions packed into a well-presented, readable book, well worth buying for the chance it gives to think again about the way we connect, not only with God but our daily lives.'
Ian Gibson, thegoodbookstall.org.uk

'This book will make your life less comfortable and your quiet times a lot more memorable. It is a brave, fresh offering from one of today's emerging creative thinkers and it will certainly stimulate you to be more active and less passive in your study of the Bible.'
Youthwork magazine (Pick of the Month, September 2006)

To Michael
On your baptism
love
Kevin & Liz

GOD 360°

120 experiential devotionals

Andy Flannagan

Visit **www.god360.co.uk**
to read about other people's god360 experiences,
share your own stories and pictures,
or listen to the god360 podcasts

Copyright © 2006 Andy Flannagan

12   11   10   09   08   07   06   8   7   6   5   4   3   2
Reprinted 2006

First published 2006 by Spring Harvest Publishing Division and Authentic Media
9 Holdom Avenue, Bletchley, Milton Keynes, Bucks,
MK1 1QR, UK
285 Lynnwood Avenue, Tyrone, GA 30290, USA
OM Authentic Media, Medchal Road, Jeedimetla Village, Secunderabad 500 055, A.P.
www.authenticmedia.co.uk
Authentic Media is a division of Send The Light Ltd., a company limited by guarantee
(registered charity no. 270162)

The right of Andy Flannagan to be identified as the Author of this Work has been asserted by
him in accordance with the Copyright, Designs and
Patents Act 1988.

British Library Cataloguing in Publication Data

A catalogue record for this book is available from the British Library

ISBN 1-85078-687-9

Unless otherwise stated, all Scripture quotations are taken from the HOLY BIBLE, NEW
INTERNATIONAL VERSION. Copyright © 1973, 1978, 1984 by the International Bible Society.
Used by permission of Hodder & Stoughton Limited. All rights reserved. 'NIV' is a registered
trademark of the International Bible Society UK Trademark number 1448790; THE MESSAGE.
Copyright © 1993, 1994, 1995, 1996, 2000, 2001, 2002. Used by permission of NavPress
Publishing Group

Cover design by fourninezero design.
Illustrated by Abi Spendlove
Print Management by Adare Carwin
Printed in Great Britain by J.H. Haynes & Co., Sparkford

Acknowledgements

The single name on the cover of a book is always shorthand for the horde of people who have been involved in making it happen. So before anything else, I really want to thank the following people: Stephanie Heald, Kate John, Ali Hull, all the ONE members, all my housegroup, Phil Grieve and Chervonne Hopkinson, Tim Hewitt, Barry Mason, Jude Smith, Ben and Esther Stansfield, Tom and Sylvia Flannagan, Steve and Joy Johnston and Lucy Payne. Thanks especially to Abi Spendlove for the phenomenal illustrations that seemed to capture exactly what was in my head. As ever, I am indebted to Roy Crowne and the British Youth For Christ family for their encouragement, love, accountability and support. I don't take it for granted.

Andy Flannagan

About the author

Andy Flannagan is British Youth For Christ's national songwriter/performer and worship leader. He does exactly what it says on the tin, except he also trains and resources people all over the UK to do the same.

Andy has a God-given passion to communicate, and that led him to leave his job as a hospital doctor in Northern Ireland to run YFC's itinerant band, TVB, for 3 years. Since then he has been regularly performing, speaking and leading worship at events like Spring Harvest, Summer Madness, Greenbelt and New Wine, pioneering a creative and experiential approach to connecting with God. His songs have been used on BBC TV and radio and he even admits to a performance on the Big Breakfast. The last few years have seen, in Andy's words 'God taking me beyond my guitar' to the forefront of developing and implementing innovative worship and devotional ideas.

2004 saw the release of his critically acclaimed album SON ('A creative triumph from the versatile Mr Flannagan.' Tony Cummings, Cross Rhythms Magazine), followed by the book Distinctive Worship. Author Nick Page described it thus, 'a breath of fresh air. Challenging, stimulating, provocative and packed with great ideas, this is a book that calls us to reshape our worship; to tread new paths and try new approaches to help people of all ages truly connect with God.'

His attitude that we are called to 'write next year's headlines by what we do today' sums up the desire in him to see Christians shape a culture rather than simply create their own. Throw in a passion for global justice, voiced through his work with Tearfund, songs with a political edge that have bent the ears of MPs, and a large dollop of playing cricket, and you have a pretty good taste of Andy's life.

www.andyflan.com

CONTENTS

FOREWORD

Watch out! This book should carry some kind of Government Health Warning. Turn the pages and before you know it Andy Flannagan will have you washing your neighbour's car, delaying your daily shower, reading books in graveyards and wandering around your local Accident and Emergency ward. The Pied Piper of Flannagan will lead you up escalators in the wrong direction, through blackberry bushes when there's a perfectly good footpath nearby and into your local Toys R Us for a time of worship. He'll even urge you to try a self-imposed power-cut.

Along comes Flan with this incendiary little book....Without so much as a 'by your leave' he hijacks the entire devotional genre in the name of Jesus, inviting each one of us to join him on a 360 degree encounter with prayer that is disturbing, demanding, occasionally funny and above all just devastatingly normal.

Normality is so often the dwelling place of God. This boring job, these screaming kids, those places and people I no longer see, still bristle and brim with God's goodness. It is religion that blinds me and when it does it is people like Andy Flannagan that come along and remind me how to live and what I must do to be saved. Andy reflects the new breed of lead-worshippers in that he is continually seeking to bring people into a conscious awareness of the presence of God – no matter where they happen to be. He leads worship on platforms to thousands of people with a guitar in hand but he also leads worship anonymously in day-to-day life, seeking to celebrate Jesus wherever he is – even amidst those primary-coloured aisles of delight called Toys R Us. The ancients described this approach as 'practicing the presence of God' at all times. People like Andy teach us how to live a life of 24-7 prayer.

On Pentecost Sunday 2005 more than 220 million people in at least 156 nations joined together for the first ever Global Day of Prayer. That's never happened before in history. A few weeks ago I was in Aarau, Switzerland, helping launch a year of unbroken, night-and-day prayer across the Italian, German and French speaking cantons. Once again, that's never happened before. What's more, if the surveys are right, even the man-in-the-street who's given up on church still believes in prayer.

But how do we actually do it? How do we grow in prayer? How do we develop a devotional life of active conversation with God without kissing our brains goodbye?

The thing I appreciate so much about this book is that it helps turn prayer from a big, fat, dutiful 'should' into a life-changing 'could'. Andy Flanagan takes us on an extraordinary journey of discovery into new dimensions of conversation with God. He helps us to encounter Christ in fresh ways by making full use of our five senses and our daily experiences. He helps us celebrate and participate in the startling sacraments of daily routine. Here we have a book – a spirituality – that really can help ordinary people like you and me get connected with God in prayer. And it seems to me that that is one of the most important things any book could possibly do.

Two thousand years ago a bunch of ordinary men decided it was high time they finally cracked the prayer thing. 'Teach us to pray' they asked Jesus. They'd seen him chatting to the Father and they knew by now that these times of devotion were the key to his whole life. They wanted to learn to pray and it all had to begin with an honest admission that they needed help. These men went on to have very significant devotional lives: They prayed on the day of Pentecost and the church was born. They prayed until rooms physically shook. They prayed Peter out of prison. They prayed and got life-changing visions. Ultimately they even prayed for their persecutors and went to their deaths. These men went on to rewrite history through the extraordinary power unlocked when they learned how to see God everywhere and to hear his whisper louder than the baying crowds.

By God's grace and humour I find myself one of the leaders of quite a big prayer movement and yet I'm still not at all good at devotional disciplines. Andy's book reminds me that there's no such thing as a distraction in prayer. Most things carry the thumbprint of the one I seek. And so, like those first disciples, I often find myself asking Jesus for practical help in prayer. I thank God for the helpful resources and brilliant ideas bursting out of Andy's imagination and out of the pages of this timely book because I believe they are also bursting from the heart of God.

Anyone seen my Bible? I'm off to Toys R Us!

Pete Greig
Chichester, England February 2006

PREFACE

Word made flesh

Sarx is the Greek word for flesh. In the Greek, it doesn't just refer to our skin, organs and muscles but the sum total of everything we are: our spirits, minds and bodies. So when John told us that, in Jesus, the 'Word became flesh', he was letting us know that Jesus was stepping into the fullness of humanity's experience. It is the miraculous transition of 'the Word' becoming flesh in our lives that is at the heart of this book. I long to see the words of the Bible fleshed out by Jesus' now body – us. For so long, in our private lives of devotion, we have been happy simply to read the words, rather than letting them become flesh in our imaginations, action and experience.

Life Experience

'It was an experience that changed my life.' We hear that phrase so often it has almost become a cliché. But it is no less powerful for that. After all, a cliché is simply something that is so widely used, it has become a victim of its own success. Let me suggest a theory. I'll bet you hear that phrase more often than 'reading those words changed my life.'

I actually did have an experience that changed my life. It happened at church, during the sermon. Except I was doing the sermon, and the sermon mostly consisted of a game of hide and seek. I wanted to unearth our attitudes to seeking God, by revealing people's attitudes to 'seeking' in general. While everyone was praying before the sermon, I slipped out, leaving only a laptop on my seat. After some perplexity the church members realised that they had to solve various clues to find me. Attitudes to the exercise ranged from childlike enthusiasm to couch potato apathy.

On my return, we used a meditation based on Bible verses about seeking and questions such as: Can we really be bothered seeking any more, or do we expect everything on a plate? Do we want the view from the top of the hill but not the climb? How does our attitude to seeking change when things aren't going so well? It had a profound impact on us. Truth had been revealed as we had experienced something together. I kept receiving text messages for days and weeks afterwards from folks telling me that they were looking for God in places that they normally wouldn't. The truth was – so was I. It changed me. It felt as if my faith had shifted from Robbie Williams to Elvis – from Let me entertain you to A little less conversation, a little more action, please.

It got me thinking and experimenting. What you find in these pages is the fruit of that journey. These are not experiences for experience' sake, but experiences that bring knowing in the reading and the doing. We hear much about trying to shift the church from 'maintenance' mode to 'mission' mode, returning us to our true calling. But as individuals we are the church, and if the devotional life of most individuals is in academic 'maintenance' mode, multiply that by a large number, and you find out where the church is. No clever macro-church program can change that. If I am honest, my devotions just felt like 'maintenance' a lot of the time.

So I resolved to look for more places of connection between God's word and God's world. I was looking for a new country that I could intentionally visit, hoping it would have a profound impact on me and those who share my journey with me. Sure, at the beginning I had to learn a new language and suffer some embarrassing moments, like any traveller, but on my return I realised that I had some great photos to share. I hope you enjoy flicking through the album.

PROLOGUE

More than words

Matthew 7:24
> Therefore everyone who hears these words of mine and puts them into practice is like a wise man who built his house on the rock.

Matthew 7:26
> But everyone who hears these words of mine and does not put them into practice is like a foolish man who built his house on sand.

Make a list of the five most significant events of your life in the past year. Stop reading. Actually do it. (You might as well get used to this now.) What makes them memorable? Let me guess at some of the ingredients of those events: risk, surprise, people you love, intense emotion, beauty? How am I doing?

So why do we forget so much of what we learn about God? Could it be that we are blindly hoping that we will remember it from safe, solitary, academic studying?

Jesus was a master at creating moments which I am certain the disciples never forgot. Imagine being at the Last Supper. A heady mix of awe, tension, reverence, fear, food and wine. Jesus makes a point of using what, for the time, were the basic building blocks of fellowship – bread and wine – as a continuing earthly reminder of heavenly intervention. There is no better example of the use of 'stuff of earth' to underline the truth. This breaking of bread was so symbolically powerful that I doubt any of the disciples were ever able to break bread again without thinking of that moment, reinforced by the sight of Jesus' broken body on a cross a few hours later.

Why has this momentous meal endured for so long as a testament to Jesus' sacrifice? Firstly, Jesus did not simply speak a set of words to the disciples. He created an experience that interacted with all their senses – they touched, they smelt, they tasted, they saw and they heard. Secondly, this was an everyday meal, with everyday ingredients, that could be repeated regularly. Surely this informs our thinking about the visual imagery that Jesus would use if present with us in bodily form today. He would not be looking for the complex sanctified icon but the simple, profound analogies hidden behind our everyday lives and the objects therein.

Whether it's in the deep symbolism of the Passover meal or the Tabernacle, you can see how far God goes to create experiential learning events for his people. There is discipline and remembrance involved. He takes great care to detail the methods and regulations involved in such key memorial events. You could also note the calming of the storm or the transfiguration as examples of Jesus allowing his disciples to learn through sharing experiences with him.

We all remember events more vividly and attach emotional significance to them if we have not simply observed but participated in them. This is especially true if we have stepped outside of our normal patterns to do it. In his book, Experiential Storytelling,[1] Mark Miller says that 'The frontiers of worship lie in helping post-moderns move, breathe deeply, express emotion, and touch the divine. Post-modern leaders create in the church an "experience economy".' He later confesses that we are ill-equipped to cope with the modern to post-modern paradigm shift: 'I learned in seminary how to craft sermons. I am not learning how to craft experiences.'

So what you have here is a set of experiences. Parts of God's big story that you can step into, not just read. You may find yourself praying for your town from the top of a multi-storey car park, as Moses and Aaron did (minus the car park) or you may find yourself meditating on what it meant for Jesus to wash his disciples' feet while washing your neighbour's car (that's our twenty-first century mode of transport).

Knowing and doing

In their excellent book Colossians Remixed,[2] Brian Walsh and Sylvia Keesmat talk in depth not just about how we apply biblical texts but how we read them. We seem to have become stuck in a 'learn, then do' mindset, which is not where many of our heads or hearts live any more. They say

> It is not simply a matter of growing in knowledge and then displaying the practical consequences or uses of that knowledge in our daily lives. No, that would be too much like the intellectualism that was the

hallmark of modernity. The knowledge and cultural fruitfulness we are talking about feed off each other. Knowing the world in wisdom and discernment engenders a certain way of life that leads to an increase in knowledge. Knowing grows in the doing.

It is this cycle of knowing growing in the doing, which in turn feeds more doing, (and vice versa) that this book is attempting to engineer. When our knowing becomes separated from any doing, we are merely academics commentating on a game that we will never really play in. When our doing becomes separated from our knowing, we have become machines, carrying out our first programmed instructions.

The reality

You might suggest that rather than crafting intentional experiences, we could simply embrace any experiences that might come our way. The problem is that I am pretty lazy – until someone makes me do something, I often don't do it. I need discipline. Deadlines help me get things done. When it comes to 'Christian' stuff we somehow get all woolly and accepting of mediocrity. We don't set any targets, because that way we won't be disappointed if we don't reach them. As the classic website www.despair.com puts it, we are 'increasing success by lowering expectations'. That's why many of these suggested activities in the book are unashamedly specific. We love half-doing things. Like the control freaks we have become, it means we can get what we want out of a situation without giving ourselves fully to it. I think, in fact, I know from grim experience that this way of living limits the space God can take in our lives.

You may say 'I want to flow with the Spirit, rather than do something prescribed for me' but the truth is that sometimes we have to open our mouths and start talking before God fills in the words. This is about those first words or first actions. Only when we build a rhythm of putting our faith into action and stepping out of comfort zones do we live lives that are open to seeing the potential for God to move in any situation.

At the end of the day, we are all creatures of habit, and I have found 'waiting for the spontaneous', to be both a cop-out and plain lazy. It sounds oxymoronic, but we have to get into the habit of being spontaneous, not for the sake of it but so we can be about our Father's business. That is why many of the suggestions of this book are about forming good habits. We happily acquiesce to a rhythm when studiously forming bad habits, but suddenly become free spirits when presented with the idea of starting a good habit.

Good habits usually only have the space to grow in the context of accountable relationships, in which we know someone will be checking up on us and asking if we have done something. Is this already sounding a bit too radical for you? Are you reaching that 'actually I'll find an easier devotional book' moment? I challenge you to take a leap of faith that will stretch your faith. We're raising the bar. Life is too short. There is too much beauty to discover and share. There is too much need that needs you. Let's take the journey together.

Devotions

Do you struggle to keep up-to-date with daily devotionals? My personal pathetic excuse is that they have always been too passive for my taste. I am more likely to do something if I have to plan it slightly and make it an event. There is then an intentionality about the time I am spending with God. I also think God notices the difference when we specifically set aside time to be with him rather than simply trundling through our usual sleepy readings.

The other regular complaint that I hear from folks is that you may well diligently read your daily devotional guide every day for a month, but if after thirty days someone asked you what you had learned, it would all be a bit of a mush. Each day fails to stand out from the others. Now, I know that it is not all about memory and that the daily 'washing of the word' is a spiritual discipline that has a positive effect on our lives, whether it reaches a conscious mental level or not, but why leave it at that? Time after time, as we have experimented with experiential learning, you find that people remember passages and concepts because they can say, oh yes – that was the day when we lit a fire, or got to the top of the car park. Not only does this build up a library of firm memories but it creates a real-world faith that means we have spiritual associations popping into our heads the next time we are involved in the activity that was part of the devotion (e.g. doing the dishes or walking in the park).

Like me, you probably don't like people telling you to do things. I don't mind people suggesting that I read things, because then I retain some control. But telling me what to do? It makes me feel like I'm back in my youth group again. You know, that might not necessarily be a bad thing. If you're anything like me, back then, you probably had a healthier attitude to learning and letting that learning influence your lifestyle. As adults we like to think that we have it sorted and that any obvious attempt at discipline would be an admission of the failure of our way of doing things (perish the thought). To be honest, I have a sobering observation – the present way of doing things isn't working. Not for me and not for most of my peers. The moments when I have noticed change effected in my own life are those moments when I have allowed God to speak to me through his word while I have processed, meditated and ruminated on it through some form of activity.

A cautionary note – this is definitely not about replacing stillness in God's presence for manic activity – I've been trying that all my life, and it doesn't work. It's about making full use of all the resources God has given us for interacting and learning about him. After all, the disciples weren't exactly bookish. We often forget that for most of church history not many people had their own Bible. Only in the last a hundred years or so has that even become a possibility. Somehow everyone still lived Christian lives before then, experiencing God through community reading and action. Is Bible reading just one more thing that we have privatised?

Don't get me wrong. I love reading Bible stories and the great illustrative stories that devotional writers tell as much as the next person. They have informed many of my opinions and attitudes. But I want more. I don't want to just read the story. I want to be part of the story – God's big story, and hopefully this book will provide you with many 'access points' where you can step into the story. You see the story of God is organic and evolving. It changes because you've started to play your part.

Activism

Some of the activities will seem unusual, or 'out-of-the-box', but the world will never change by people doing things 'normally', within the social constraints decided for us by our 'each to their own' society. Living in direct opposition to the spirit and culture of their time is what got the early church noticed, and extended the borders of a radical Kingdom.

There have recently been a spate of books like 365 ways to change your world, which are fantastic resources for activism in many areas. The problem with these sort of books is however perfectly illustrated by my friend Phil, who is by no means a couch potato.

'Flan, I feel guilty and depressed. Help!' I had bumped into him in a bookshop as he was flicking through a book like this. Even a few minutes' glancing had made him feel physically sick. I flicked to page 11 and spotted the problem. There was a list of 'the ten things that you will need' to change the world, and number five was 'Unconditional love for others 24/7 – essential.' There was no indication where one was supposed to find it. Without a power source from outside of ourselves, attempts at changing the world, though noble in intent, either last for about a month or eventually leave you in an even more frustrated and cynical place than when you started. Hopefully this book will give you the ideas and the spiritual resources to enable you to do them.

Practicalities

We will carry out some of the activities as individuals, some as small groups and some as local communities. Some will be carried out by a nationwide community via the web. Some will involve prayer, some will involve service, some will involve silence. Some will pamper you, and some will stretch you.

Some of the suggestions may appear quite immediate but I always find that if I haven't acted on something within the first 24 hours of opportunity, the chances are that I won't act on it at all. That's just the reality of our lives. What is helpful for you will take root and grow and what is not will wither and die. That's OK. Some will be impossible for logistical reasons. We can't all do everything but let's at least do something and the best way to start is simply starting.

Some you won't finish in one day. Some you'll come back to again and again. Some will be over before they've started. One day is not necessarily finished when you turn the page. This doesn't have to be sequential experience. We are not talking about a daily duty but random moments of intentional God interaction. Do you remember the 'Choose your own adventure' books of the 80s? In these, the paragraphs were all numbered and you had to make decisions about whether your character would walk east or west, fight or flee, speak or scream. Each decision sent you to a different numbered paragraph. They were fantastic. The books were crafted in such a way that you felt as if you were deciding your own fate, though I always seemed to end up at the same dead ends. Sometimes it took the twelfth or thirteenth read of the book to get to the end of the maze or dungeon (even with cheating). Please feel the same freedom to browse through the devotions. None of your lives will be the same, so you will need to construct your own unique course through these ideas. For example, there may be times when you are nowhere near a car or a town, when either is required. Just skip on to the next one. You can come back some day.

I was watching a film at the Tate Gallery in Liverpool recently and one phrase just jumped out at me – 'These days something has to be consumed before it has 'happened" – e.g. I haven't properly experienced the concert until I have sent a blurred picture to someone else's phone. The great goal I scored isn't really valuable until I share the story with the guys back home. Hopefully we will be able to use some of this dynamic as we share our stories and pictures (via the website www.god360.co.uk), of what happened when we got off our seats and did something.

It should be pointed out that these devotions are not intended as a comprehensive daily Bible reading course. Yes, some sections will follow a narrative but by their nature, many of the activities focus in on one strong action or learning point. I am not for a moment saying that this is the most important or the only learning point from a passage.

Aside from the instructions in each devotion, I recommend that you read each passage slowly, praying and meditating on the words. Well take that as read! (Quite literally!)

Exercise

The word 'exercise' quite well describes some of the experiences in the book as there is innate value in physical exercise for its own sake, but it also prepares you for more sustained activity 'in the heat of battle', such as a hockey or rugby game. It is in the nature of such exercises that they are prescriptive or repetitive, but without the training, we end up gasping for air when we take to the pitch.

How can you swim counter-culturally when the tide is flowing so strongly against you? Only by doing the intensive daily training that a cross-channel swimmer does. Yes, it's tough but who ever promised it would be easy? It's obvious but you need to practise being counter-cultural to be able to do it consistently.

Just knowing the 'good that I should do' is not good enough. We all know the worrying facts about our world – whether it's the ever-growing divide between rich and poor, or the escalating racial and religious tensions. We all know the hurt and pain that is all around us in our communities. The gap seems to exist between knowing and doing anything about it. Even Paul said, 'I have the desire to do what is good, but I cannot carry it out.' (Rom. 7:18)

As a teenager, the quantum leaps that I made in learning French did not happen behind a desk in a classroom, but on family holidays in the campsites and villages of Brittany. The phrases I learnt and used regularly there are the ones that I can still recall now. It's not that my time in the classroom was wasted. It formed a vital foundation of understanding. But without putting this concept into practice where it was subject to scrutiny, it remained a blunt tool. Have we spent too much time in the classroom and not enough time on the streets with God? Real learning that lasts happens through experience. Many types of experiential learning are fast becoming acknowledged methods in various professional disciplines. Hang on. It feels as if I've heard all this before somewhere. Oh yeah . . .

> "Why do you call me, 'Lord, Lord,' and do not do what I say? I will show you what he is like who comes to me and hears my words and puts them into practice. He is like a man building a house, who dug down deep and laid the foundation on rock. When the flood came, the torrent struck that house but could not shake it, because it was well built. But the one who hears my words and does not put them into practice is like a man who built a house on the ground without a foundation. The moment the torrent struck that house, it collapsed and its destruction was complete" (Lk. 6:46-49: italics mine).

Impact

I honestly believe that enough of us praying and doing these things together could change the world.

You may think you cannot change the world but you do have some control over you. People ask me why the world is in the state it is and I usually reply like this. How much control of my life does God have? Forty percent, fifty percent perhaps? – the truth is, as much as I let him and therein lie all the mixed motivations, selfish moments, and ensuing heartbreak. Just multiply that up by six billion and you actually get quite an accurate picture of the world – all its hurts, conflicts and injustices. Why do we believe that, when you look at the big picture, everyone else will be different to us?

I once read the story of a New York taxi driver who would go out of his way to be courteous, helpful and encouraging to his passengers. At the time, this was definitely a counter-cultural effort. One shocked passenger asked him why he was doing this, and he replied 'I'm changing the world!' His passenger questioned whether this was actually possible and he explained, 'I am. I'm changing the world one person at a time. If I'm kind to a passenger, and cheer her up, then if she's a schoolteacher she will treat her kids well this morning, and they will enjoy their day. When they come home happy, they will brighten up their parents' day, which means that they may well be kind to their neighbours or the folks who call at the door. You see, joy spreads. And I get a chance to start a new ripple of joy about every fifteen minutes.' His passenger got out the car with a spring in his step, ready to surf the wave.

Margaret Mead, the American anthropologist, said this, 'Never doubt that a small group of committed citizens can change the world. Indeed it is the only thing that ever has.'[3]

The past

If these ideas have their roots anywhere, it is probably in the ancient Celtic traditions with their daily rhythms of prayer. In communities and monasteries, prayer was woven into the very fabric of daily life, with prayers for washing, eating, gardening etc. There was a strong sense that God was not restricted to the 'Holy places' that were made of human hands. The words of St. Patrick's prayer (commonly called 'St. Patrick's breastplate') confirm this.

Christ with me, Christ before me, Christ behind me
Christ in me, Christ beneath me, Christ above me
Christ on my right, Christ on my left
Christ when I lie down, Christ when I sit down, Christ when I arise
Christ in the heart of every man who thinks of me
Christ in the mouth of everyone who speaks of me
Christ in every eye that sees me
Christ in every ear that hears me

The future

The cynics could rightly note that not a lot changes from a one-off event. As Andrew Marr correctly said on the day of the Live8 concerts, 'Some of these people are part of a movement, but most of them want to be part of a moment.'

My prayer therefore is not that you become dependent on 'experiential devotions' for the rest of your life. That would perhaps bless my publishers but it is not my intent. My hope is that these ideas will kick-start your own creative engines to craft worshipful, practical, world-changing, learning experiences for yourself and the people with whom you journey. And that these experiences would lead to the Word literally becoming flesh in your life and your world.

Getting personal

Each of the devotions have been tried out by me, and by some of my very kind friends in Luton and further afield. (Thanks to you all for your help and feedback.) If you give them a chance, and actually do them, (not just read them like a browsing shopper) they do work. And I'll tell you what is more exciting for me than seeing them all in a book. It's the fact that they are changing me. I have honestly been a different human since these concepts started creeping into my everyday life. I walk around differently. I rush less. I see God in places I never expected to see him, probably because I am looking for him. Every sound, building or conversation becomes an opportunity to encounter God. I've decided that 'practising the presence of God' isn't about hiding yourself away so there's nothing else to think about (even though that is a vital discipline at times) and more about allowing God's Spirit to weave himself into every moment of touch, taste, smell, sight and sound as well as impacting your spirit.

There is another important dynamic here. Through our devotional lives, we seek to get to know Jesus better day by day. For as long as this 'getting to know' is confined to historical recall or private prayer, we are only seeing certain aspects of who he is. Anyone who works in the deprived parts of this world will tell you that they meet Jesus there. They see him in the faces and hands of the poor and the oppressed. They see him healing the sick, releasing the oppressed, bringing sight to the blind and proclaiming good news to the poor. We meet him in the doing. He doesn't ask us to help because he needs our help. He asks us to help him so we can be where he is and truly get to know him.

John said that Jesus came 'full of grace and truth.' Jesus said 'I am the truth.' Learning the truth is not like learning an objective set of facts. We have shrunk it to be something smaller than the living, breathing thing that it is; truth is fleshed out in a person. To meet this truth, you have to meet it in the flesh. Without 'fleshing out' this incarnate truth in our communities, we don't really 'know it' either. As Brian Walsh and Sylvia Keesmat put it, 'In this respect, seeing (experiencing, touching and feeling) is indeed believing.'

Warning: This book will annoy you. If you use it properly, it will make your life less comfortable but I guarantee that you'll also feel more alive than you ever have. Enjoy the adventure!

AF

Visit the website at **www.god360.co.uk** to read about other people's god360 experiences, share your own stories and pictures, or listen to the god360 podcasts.

SEASON 1

PART 1: COLOSSIANS

1

STATING THE OBVIOUS

Read Colossians 1:1-6

I love the fact that sometimes the Bible just tells us what we already know. I know that 'all over the world the Gospel is bearing fruit' and that it is doing the same in me; but I constantly need reminding. When my eyes only take in what is served up for me on TV and I gaze at my navel without God's spectacles, I forget that all of what we have just read is actually true, right here, right now. This is the beauty of the Word of God. This is why our daily 'washing with the word', which echoes the laver ritual from tabernacle times (Ex. 30:17-21) is so important.

We need to reclaim the word 'reality.' This is reality. God's version is the version. It's the physical, temporary stuff that is often fake. We are not physical beings having temporary spiritual experiences. We are spiritual beings having a temporary physical experience.

Paul is building up his readers by speaking the truth to them. I fear that we sometimes neglect saying the obvious, either because we're too lazy, too cool or we're off looking for something incredibly clever and post-modern to say. We all need to hear the simple, obvious stuff from each other, every day.

- You are chosen by God.
- Jesus will never let you go.
- I cherish you.
- His spirit comforts you.
- Your life is bearing fruit.
- You are a temple of the Holy Spirit.
- You are so important to me.
- God is doing great things in you.
- God is doing great things through you.
- The Kingdom is coming in Luton (insert town name appropriately).

These things are all true, whether we choose to see them or not. Speaking them to each other increases the likelihood that we will believe them and that they will change how we live.

Send 'truth-telling' sentences to ten people via email today. Be bold. Remember some of them will seem too obvious to say. Go through the pain barrier. The recipients will need to hear them. You might want to use Bible verses. It might start a revolution in how we talk to each other. Our conversations and emails may start sounding a little less 'Vicky' and a little bit more 'Paul-ine'.

NOTES

2

INPUT

Get out as many old photo albums as you can find, and browse through them for a while. Enjoy the memories of the relationships represented there.

Now read **Colossians 1:7-14**.

Who have you learned the truth from? Perhaps using the photos as an aide-memoire, make a list of the key individuals in your life who have influenced you by their words and deeds. Beside their name, detail what their major impact was – perhaps it was simply one statement or their strength in a particular area. These people may not even be folks that you know well. It could be someone you once heard speak at an event or whose story inspired you.

Now let them know. I had the privilege of connecting two people last year, where a young girl owed her escape from a shocking lifestyle to a youth worker friend of mine. The youth worker had moved away before this girl had got it together enough to say thanks but a random meeting and two emails later, something very beautiful had happened. It may take some effort to track people down but web searches make this a much easier task than it used to be. You will be amazed how encouraged people will be by what you tell them. Sometimes it is all the more special because there has been a substantial time lag.

On another tack, who prays for you? You may be surprised how many people do pray for you. Usually once folks have connected with you in a significant way, you stay in their hearts and minds, as with Paul and the Colossians in the passage. Is there a group of people that you regularly share information about your life with? If not, assemble an email, text or physical group who can regularly pray for you. Remember prayer is not just for negative situations. So often we only employ the might of God's people on their knees when we're in crisis mode. We miss out on the blessings and impact that may come when we also invite people to pray into our joys and successful areas, for the deepening and widening of our gifts or for ears to hear the Spirit's prompting in life situations. This anomaly also feeds our false belief that, in the successful times, we are achieving what we achieve through our own efforts.

Our housegroup has a 'prayer chain', whereby a prayer request is texted to the next person in the loop, who then passes it on. All I need to remember is which person is after me in the loop and twelve people are praying on the issue within a very short space of time. I have resolved to make sure that I send as many 'offensive' requests as 'defensive' requests, so we will be on the attack in our prayers and not just fire-fighting.

Sort out who your sisters and brothers-in-arms will be.

NOTES

3

OUTPUT

Buy a new photo album.

Unusually, we are using the same passage as the previous devotion, but before you read it again, I have two questions:

Who is learning the truth from you?
Who are you praying for?

Now read the passage (**Colossians 1:7-14**) in light of those questions.

For both questions, it's list time again. It's great every once in a while to take stock and analyse whom you are impacting with your life. Check how much cross-over there is between today's and yesterday's lists. I fear that a lot of my prayers for other people only happen reactively rather than in a structured intentional way. If I really want to impact others with my life, then that will start with praying for them. Otherwise I end up banging my head against a spiritual brick wall with an earthly head. One practical idea is to scroll through your mobile phone phone book, and pray sequentially for those listed. You can do this any time, any place, anywhere. Paul says they had 'not stopped' praying for the Colossians.

Over the coming days and weeks find (or take) photos of those you are already impacting, or whom you are resolving to impact. Obviously this may not be appropriate in some circumstances and, if so, simply write the names and prayers in a book. Build up a new album that is more about looking forward than looking back, that is more about you giving than receiving, and which reminds you to regularly pray for these people.

NOTES

4

LOST AND FOUND

Colossians 1:13-14

Give a precious item that you own to a local charity shop or 'cash converters' store. It doesn't need to be something expensive – just something that has sentimental value to you or will be hard to replace. If you're struggling to think of anything, just have a quick look around your bedroom or living room or, for the most effective method, ask a friend or your spouse to choose. They'll know what will really mean something to you. If you're still really struggling, as a soft option, you could just choose your favourite CD or DVD.

In the next one to two days, experience what it felt like for God to 'let go' of us, running the risk that we may never return. We enjoy having freewill, but any of you who are parents will know that, at times, you would rather cancel your offspring's freewill for a day or two, to save them from themselves. However, the remarkable truth is that the story doesn't end there. God buys us back.

Walk to the shop for the second time, mirroring God's 'rescue mission', and as you do, ask God to reveal to you the scale of his love for his children who have not yet returned.

You won't know whether your item will still be there, or whether it will have been snaffled up by a bargain hunter. Experience the tension. This is the tension that God must experience in giving us freewill. As you buy the item back you might experience a sense of injustice in having to pay for something that is actually yours, but that is what God did for us.

Hebrews 9:12
> He did not enter by means of the blood of goats and calves; but he entered the Most Holy Place once for all by his own blood, having obtained eternal redemption.

It is that word 'redemption' that we have been fleshing out here. In these days of multiple kidnappings, we are sadly all too aware of what a ransom is. It is quite literally given in exchange for someone's life. The money you paid in the above exercise was a ransom for your precious item. With the item safe in your possession, reflect on the fact that God's economy doesn't allow for simple cash conversion. The currency of this transaction is blood.

If the item has been snapped up by an avid Spice Girls fan, then you are going to experience something of the pain of a Father that let his son depart with half the inheritance. Let this longing to have what was once yours safely restored change your heart and prayers for those who you know are still 'in a faraway land'. If we even knew a fraction of his pain, I think it would change our praying lives forever.

NOTES

5

FOCUS IN

To produce an image, all you need is a lens, a light source and something to focus the image on. So get a piece of paper and a lens of some sort (probably some spectacles) and go outside to find the sun (apologies to readers in Northern Ireland). Attempt to create a tiny image of the sun on your piece of paper. Resist the temptation to incinerate small creatures.

Now read **Colossians 1:15-20**. Christ was the 'image of the invisible God'.

Your Physics teacher may have told you that an image is a two-dimensional representation of a three-dimensional object. Whether that is on a movie screen, or in your photo album, real experiences are made more accessible. Now we need to watch our language here, because Jesus was fully God, but as he stepped down a dimension or seven to become human, he became a touchable, accessible representation of God – 'the image of the invisible God'. The Greek here (eikon) speaks of an exact representation which is drawn from the object, not merely a resemblance. But just as earlier you could only produce an image of the sun on paper if you tilted the angle of the lens correctly, this reality was only possible because Jesus continually had the lens of his life orientated in the right direction. It was always pointed at God. The challenging part of all this is that we are also called to be images of God. But is your lens pointing in the right direction to collect God's light or is it orientated mostly towards the things of this world, merely creating images of them?

Keep a note today of who you orientate yourself towards. Whose appearance would make you cut short a phone call? Who would you cancel a meeting for? Is it always those with power or influence? Every time you notice the sun, or feel its light and warmth, think about which direction the lens of your life is pointing. Do you feel as if you have captured any of God's light today and been an accessible, viewable image of the invisible God?

Extra time

It's easy to miss how subversive Paul is actually being in these verses. The church in Colossae lived under the shadow of the Roman empire. When Paul declares Christ's supremacy, it is in direct competition to Caesar. His image was displayed in every public place and on many household objects. The Roman empire ruled not just by force and efficiency but by the capturing of its subjects' imaginations, too. 'There is no Lord but Caesar' was the catchphrase of the empire. Paul dangerously begs to differ. We also live under an empire which makes excellent use of logos and branding to control our imaginations. Will we bow to these images or be people of another Kingdom?

NOTES

PART 1: COLOSSIANS

SEASON 1

6

WILD GOOSE CHASE

Colossians 2:6-8

Can you believe that the sentence below was written almost two thousand years ago? (Plus ça change, plus la meme...)

> See to it that no-one takes you captive through hollow and deceptive philosophy, which depends on human tradition and the basic principles of this world rather than on Christ (Col. 2:8).

Make a note of the accepted systems of speech or action that you buy into today.

You won't have to go to far before you come across them. Some examples are sarcasm, criticism, complaint, status, 'selfish' economics, relativism, celebrity, survival of the fittest or materialism. We may be riled by a conversation or action which is blatantly antagonistic to God or Christians, but for some reason the sacred-secular split in our brains causes us to miss all these others. These are actually much more subtle systems of thought and interaction that just suck the Kingdom out of the world. Paul's observation that these philosophies hold people 'captive' could not be more accurate. They place our minds in cells that don't allow any spiritual visitors and after a while we forget that there is anything beyond the four walls of cynicism, criticism, calculation and competition.

Eugene Petersen puts it like this in The Message. 'I don't want anyone leading you off on some wild-goose chase' because 'I want you woven into a tapestry of love, in touch with everything there is to know of God.

Memorise the 4 Cs of cynicism, criticism, calculation and competition. Keep an eye out for their appearance in your heart and mind. Their mission is to stop us being able to love freely. Pray for the freedom to love without cynicism, love without criticism, love without calculation, and love without competition. There might just be times when the Cs are useful, but if we're honest we'll never lose them completely, so they'll probably be there if we need them!

NOTES

7

SPIRITUAL SOAP SUDS

This devotion needs to take place before you've washed.

Read **Colossians 2:9-15**.

How many things do you wash every day? Hands, face, glasses, plates? How do you feel when you walk into a kitchen and see a pile of unwashed dishes? How do you feel in the morning before you've washed or showered? Clinging clothes and sweaty smells just make us feel bad, for some reason. We were made to be clean. It is defence number one against myriad bacteria. Washing is integral to life, no matter where you live. So it's not surprising that God chose baptism as a universal symbol of the faith.

Acts 22:16
> And now what are you waiting for? Get up, be baptised and wash your sins away, calling on his name.

James 4:8
> Come near to God and he will come near to you. Wash your hands, you sinners, and purify your hearts, you double-minded.

Revelation 22:14
> Blessed are those who wash their robes, that they may have the right to the tree of life and may go through the gates into the city.

Now have a shower or bath (if that's what you normally do).

Notice the difference. Compare how you felt before and after washing or having a shower. What difference to your attitude or confidence does it make?

So how regular is your spiritual washing? Baptism represents dying to sin and rising to life in Jesus. Bearing in mind that 'death' pretty accurately describes how many of us feel in the morning, wouldn't it be great to make this 'washing' of your life a daily discipline? Wouldn't it be great if your spiritual washing made a similar difference to how you feel?

Try to incorporate regular prayer into your showering routine. As the water hits your head for the first time, ask God to pour his Holy Spirit on you, to cleanse you from all the spiritual dirt that sticks to you. We don't even have to make bad decisions for dust to accumulate in our lives. It's an inevitable consequence of being in contact with a fallen world. Washing, dusting and cleaning are things you just have to do.

NOTES ●◆

THINK UP

The next verses summarise some of the implications of our baptism.

Read **Colossians 3:1-11.**

I love the phrase that says my life is now 'hidden with Christ in God.' Stop for a moment and simply meditate on that phrase. What does it conjure up for you? The immense safety of that concept is phenomenal. The word used for 'hidden' here has the sense of a planted seed, which is alive but preparing for true life. Our spiritual lives are in a sense 'underground', but then 'appear with him in glory.'

If, as these verses say, we have died and then been raised, then our preoccupation with the temporary things of this world makes no sense. But 'Set your heart on things above' is still a challenging statement. How much time do we spend thinking about things of heaven, compared to the time we spend thinking about 'things of earth'?

Is the time when your brain focuses on 'things above' limited to a 'quiet time' slot or do 'things above' pervade every situation? To be honest, even in a quiet time I can quite easily be simply asking God to focus his attention on my 'things of earth', rather than me focusing on his things above.

Are your to-do lists (the outflow of your thinking) all about earthly matters, or also about heavenly concerns? Would an observer of our lives know that we believe there is something beyond this world?

From my experience, focusing on deleting the 'things of earth' mentioned in verses 5-8 is only temporarily effective unless I am seeing them in true contrast. It's like realising that I've been watching a fuzzy picture on a black and white portable TV out of habit, because I know how it works, rather than unpacking the wide-screen home cinema sitting in the garage. After the moment of realisation, you know what happens. You'll never watch the portable again. It's much easier to get rid of it then. The same applies to our earthly habits.

Make a list on cards of some of the 'things above' that you will attempt to fix your eyes on during today. Stick the cards on the ceiling, as a reminder to keep 'thinking up.'

NOTES

9

REFINING FIRE

Colossians 3:5-8

It's very easy to read these verses and think that they don't apply to us. These verses are only for the murderers and revellers of the world, surely? On closer examination, perhaps we are more a part of the story that we might imagine. Paul is writing to the Colossian church, after all. These are words intended for people just like you and me, and please don't try and tell me that we have somehow risen to a higher moral plane in the nineteen centuries since this letter was written.

Write each of the sins listed in the passage in the centre of a piece of A4 paper (one per page). Around the word, scribble the situations where you struggle with that particular sin. Spend a decent amount of time reflecting on each one, asking God to illuminate things that have settled to the back of your mind. Ask for and receive his forgiveness.

Paul exhorts the Colossians not to file away these sins, or micro-manage them, but to 'put them to death', so dramatic action is required. Gather up your sheets of paper, find a safe spot outside and burn them. Yes, burn them. As you do, pray that the hold these things have on your life will disappear for good. If there are things that have come to light during this time, make sure you share them with someone else, so that they can help you with this part of your journey.

NOTES

10

GOD'S GARMENTS

You need to be undressed before starting this devotion.

Colossians 3:12-17

Your clothes are a choice. You choose them in a store, and on any given morning, you have a choice as to which items you put on.

Similarly, we can choose to put on the garments listed in verse 12. But so often we just dress according to our mood, almost as victims of circumstance, and we only put on the clothes such as 'compassion' if we've been overcome with some emotion or we 'feel like it'. In the physical, we have to dress up in clothes that we really don't feel like putting on for certain events but often after we've put them on, we notice that our attitude has changed. We get into 'game' mode. In the same way, sometimes we need to actively choose these spiritual garments.

As you dress yourself today, attribute each of the qualities mentioned in the passage to a piece of clothing. As you put them on, pray that you would truly be clothed with that aspect of Kingdom living. Pray for the strength to choose these attitudes today in the various situations where you will need them. Visualise those moments when, because of people or circumstances, it will be hard to be gentle or compassionate. You could let this become a morning routine. What a difference it might make to the people around you if you leave the house wearing compassion, kindness, humility, gentleness and patience everyday. You may even start a fashion trend. God is the new black.

There are also echoes here of other Scripture passages which describe the significance of the spiritual clothes we wear. As we put on these qualities they cover our nakedness and shame that we inherited from the original naked couple, Adam and Eve. The prodigal son receives the 'best robe' on returning to the father, restoring his status and dignity. In Ephesians 4, Paul also exhorts us to 'to put on the new self, created to be like God in true righteousness and holiness', similar to Joshua's change of clothes in Zechariah chapter 3. There are also the pure white robes which we read of ourselves wearing in Revelation chapter 7, which have been 'made white in the blood of the Lamb.' Take some time to check out these passages.

White will be the new black. Forever.

NOTES

PART 1: COLOSSIANS

SEASON 1

11

FINAL GREETINGS

Colossians 3:7-18

I love the 'final greetings' sections of Paul's letters. I am so glad that someone didn't remove them for the sake of efficiency. They remind us that Paul is interacting with real people and not simply posting a sermon on the internet. He is speaking directly into their situations with conviction, which has inherent risks to his relationship with them. Do we take those same risks for the good of the Kingdom? Am I more likely to point out a generic spiritual problem to a large number of people than mention it specifically to my sister or brother, who is actually struggling with it?

Another wonderful thing about these opening and closing statements is the honesty with which Paul encourages and thanks people. This is the basis for today's experience.

I have been present at many a leaving-do and funeral in my life. Genuine, beautiful words are spoken, but I am often left wondering if this is the first time that the 'leaver' has heard them (if they still can). And if so, why? Is it a fear of intimacy or is it our inbuilt competitiveness that can only build someone up once they are no longer a threat? Like the elder brother of the prodigal, we find it so hard to enjoy the blessings of others, without referencing them to our perceived lack of blessings. Can we hear the father whisper to us 'All I have is yours'?

So have a 'psychological leaving-do' for a friend or relative. Sometimes the only way to confront how we truly feel about someone and be able to express it, is to imagine what we would say if we knew we weren't going to see them for some time, or perhaps ever. Suddenly words of thanks and remorse and exhortation begin to flow. We all need the encouragement that we usually only hear at the end of a project during it as well.

This could mean a letter, a visit, a gift, or any number of creative methods of communication. However don't feel the need to tell them that you were imagining them gone, or worse, dead!

I understand the pain barrier you have to go through with this one, but 'risking in faith' is when Kingdom action tends to happen. All your peers beginning to interact in an encouraging way may well start with you.

NOTES●✧

GIVE AND TAKE

Colossians 3:15-17

Today write a psalm, hymn or spiritual song to God, which you could later share with your small group. If you're not feeling musical, then simply write a spoken psalm or poem. Is there something you have read recently in the Bible that could inspire a song and teach your small group a key truth? Or you may feel more comfortable preparing a five minute 'thought for the day' type chat, to explain what you've been learning or what you feel that your group need to hear.

If you've never done this before, all the more reason to dive in now. Verse 16 states 'Let the word of Christ dwell in you richly as you teach and admonish one another with all wisdom, and as you sing psalms, hymns and spiritual songs with gratitude in your hearts to God.' It underlines that teaching is meant to be a communal thing. We are all meant to teach each other, rather than always relying on one person to lead our thinking. Leading in these contexts can be as simple as asking everyone prepared questions, such as 'What risks did Jesus take in this story?' and 'What risks have you taken for God this week?' Bouncing thoughts and ideas inspired by the Bible back and forth is how we 'let the word of Christ dwell in you richly' rather than simply letting it visit us for a few moments, and leave again.

If you don't have a small group of some description, who are you kidding? We all like to think that the normal rules of the game somehow don't apply to us, or that we've grown out of needing that sort of stuff. But if we aren't playing out our faith with a small number of people, then where are we playing it out? I have to confess to having been part of groups because 'I felt I should' for most of my life, rather than believing that they were the living, breathing home of my faith. This is a team game, not a solo sport.

Pray that God would plant in you a desire to play your part in the teaching and admonishing of your community of believers.

NOTES

13

SALT SHAKER OR SPIN DOCTOR?

Colossians 4:1-6

Take your Bible to your kitchen. As you read the passage, dip your finger in some salt and taste it. Experience the mild discomfort as you read. Feel free to have some fruit juice ready for when you finish.

It is interesting that Paul uses the phrase 'full of grace, seasoned with salt.' This chimes with what John said about Jesus – 'he came full of grace and truth'. Yes, we must be gentle but also alert to every opportunity to insert some truth in a gracious way. Too often we believe that our job is to be 'spin doctors for the Kingdom.' We think that if we make our message acceptable enough and are nice enough to enough people, then eventually folks will think that Christians are 'dead on' and stride effortlessly towards the pearly gates. Like me, do you feel that your conversation can be pretty grace-full, but 'could do with a bit more salt'? We superimpose our desperate desire to be liked and accepted by our peers onto 'God conversations', leaving us trying to make people like and accept God. God doesn't want to be liked. He wants to be worshipped.

Pray for an opportunity to sprinkle some salt into a situation today. Taste the salt again as you do so, to remind you that the moments you are praying for may not actually be enjoyable. The salt might sting at times, but will in the end preserve lives that are imperceptibly, but definitely, rotting.

At this point, it's encouraging to note that even Paul needed prayer help for getting his foot in the door, as verse 3 shows: 'And pray for us, too, that God may open a door for our message, so that we may proclaim the mystery of Christ, for which I am in chains.'

A common icebreaker game is asking folks, 'If you were a packet of crisps, what flavour would you be?' Could it be that our words should have the same slightly shocking, but eventually pleasant impact as 'salt and vinegar'?

NOTES ●◆

SEASON 1

PART 2

14

CHANGE YOUR ALTITUDE

The Israelites have been grouchy, tired and thirsty. Poor old Moses is the lightning conductor for their complaints and believes they are about to stone him. However, God answers their question, 'Is the Lord among us?' with an emphatic 'Yes.' by providing 'Horeb springs' water. As if this wasn't enough action for one place, the Amalekites show up and they're not bearing gifts.

Exodus 17:8-15

Following Moses' example, get to the best vantage point above the area where you live. For me, this is the top of a multi-storey car park but for you it may be a tower or a nearby hill. Read the passage again. High places have enormous significance throughout the Bible. They take us above the madding crowd and give us perspective. The air is clearer and perhaps we hear God more clearly.

Pray for the spiritual battles going on in your town. Pray for the lives that are presently captive to the evil one. Pray for the churches (many of which will be in your view). If there are obvious areas of need and deprivation or darkness, then pray specifically for them. It impresses me that Moses had such commitment to pray for these people who just a few moments before had been on the point of stoning him. How often are our prayers aimed merely at those whom we like?

Ask God to lead your eyes and spirit to specific areas or issues that need some spiritual warfare. You may want to raise your hands as Moses did. My friend Keith once crafted me a beautiful prayer stick for this very purpose. (It looks like a walking stick for a giant). Something like that could come in handy. Take a picture and share it on the website www.god360.co.uk, so others can pray for your town/area too.

NOTES

15

PAY TO PRAISE

The story so far – **David has sinned by putting trust in facts and figures over faith in God**. (A bit like one of us choosing whether or not to go on a mission trip based solely on perusing our bank statements.) He has wasted time counting the number of men in his armies like a paranoid teenager playing Risk. He is given three options – three years' famine, three months' fleeing from enemies, or three days' plague. Quite an a la carte to choose from. Without phoning a friend, David goes for answer C but is appalled at the outcome, as Jerusalem is left on the point of annihilation. However, God is even more appalled and stops the angels of death at Araunah's house. He tells David to go and build an altar there to save his people.

Read **2 Samuel 24:18-25**.

I remember exactly where I was sitting when I first read verse 24. 'I will not sacrifice to the Lord my God burnt offerings that cost me nothing.' I felt immediately convicted. How many of my 'offerings' of worship cost me very little at all? For most of us, if we're honest, there is not much sacrifice involved as we actually quite like singing songs and getting that warm fuzzy feeling that comes when people get together and share a common belief and purpose.

So I challenge you today to let your time with God cost you something. Perhaps to your comfort, perhaps to your schedule, perhaps to your self-respect or perhaps to your credibility. I often challenge those who are normally seated or standing motionless in worship to dance or move and those who are normally busting their cool moves to be still and silent. Where you are, do something that costs, whether that means lying prostrate before God or singing within earshot of your neighbours.

Other ideas to get you thinking could include reading your Bible in public (not necessarily out loud), leaving a whole evening free to simply worship or visiting a church whose style of worship is very different to your own.

NOTES

SWITCH OFF, TUNE IN

Mark 9:42-50

This is a 'hardcore' passage, so deserves some uncompromising thought.
I believe that the biggest obstacle to many Christians growing in God is not
particularly theological or deep. It is rectangular and it combines sound and
vision in such a way as to numb our creative centres to the point where we
forget that we are capable of original thought. It is called television.

Do an audit of your TV watching today. Total the minutes. How much of this
time is 'quality time'? Do we interact with those around us? Is the power of
advertising and suggestive imagery taking us over without us realising it?
Is it simply a poor second best to time alone with God? Let's face it. We love
it because it is low effort. It provides all the warm fuzzy feelings of a
relationship without any of the responsibilities; all the banter of a night out,
without the fear of the joke ever being on you. The virtual families that we
become part of are better looking, richer, and more interesting than our real
ones, and they will never argue with us or demand anything from us.

So can you do without it? If not, why not? Challenge some friends to fast from
TV with you, and see how it improves your social and fellowshipping lives.
You could start with a day, then try a week, then who knows? You can get
news via the radio, newspapers and the internet. Why is it so important for
us to know everything about everything that is going on, anyway? It's not
like we do anything about it. Some of us watch 24 hour news channels as if
failing to do so would jeopardise the safety of the nation, because we don't
know a certain fact. We want to be part of the story. We want to play our part.
The trouble is that there is a bigger story that the TV doesn't even start to
show us and in fact TV often distracts us from seeing it. That bigger story is
God's story and it can't be shrunk into a rectangle.

Let's be part of that story by switching off, getting out of our seats, listening to the playwright, taking his direction and stepping onto the stage.

NOTES

17

PRACTICE MAKES PERFECT

When was the last time you shared your faith publicly? I don't necessarily mean on a street with a megaphone. When was the last time you actually articulated what it means to be a Christian to a friend or colleague? Sometimes it's helpful and confidence-giving to work out exactly what you would say if someone asked you to 'give the reason for the hope you have' (1 Pet. 3:15). Have you thought about how to share your own story? It is the one thing that no-one can dispute. Or have you thought about how to share the story of God? Check out how the martyr Stephen did this by reading Acts 7.

Book time with two Christian friends, and role-play scenarios where one of you is a Christian and two of you are not. Sit on three chairs arranged in a triangle. Take it in turns to be the Christian for fifteen minute segments. Fire questions and comments at the 'Christian'. Take a theme for each segment such as 'Sex and sexuality', 'Suffering', 'God and science', 'The Bible' or 'Other faiths'. Below are some questions to get you going. Let each others' answers and the manner in which you answer be training for the real situation. These exercises always highlight areas about which we need to know more and give us confidence in the areas where we have thought things through.

- Is it not really arrogant to say that Christianity is right and that everyone else is wrong?
- Surely you believe that because you've grown up in a Christian family or Christian country….if you'd grown up in Iran, you'd be a Muslim, wouldn't you?
- If God is a good God, how could he send anyone to hell?
- It's only the weak people I know who need God. It's like a crutch….
- The Christians I know are so annoying. They never practise what they preach.

- Surely if you live a decent life and do no-one any harm, you'd get to heaven?
- What about all the starving children in Africa? Could God not stop that if he wanted to?
- Why doesn't he then?
- So basically, God's not in control then, is he?
- Do you hear voices in your head? That's weird...
- People shouldn't force their views on others. Isn't that what causes wars?
- God can't break the laws of science, can he?
- How do you know that it hasn't all been made up?
- Is it not just like Chinese whispers? The whole story has been exaggerated through time.

Remember in the real situation, it's important to not get lost in an intellectual battle, when someone may simply need you to listen to them, or a question is merely flagging a deeper hurt or issue. For further research, I would recommend websites like www.christiananswers.net, www.josh.org and www.licc.org.

At the end, remember to encourage each other and feedback any constructive advice you have. Finish by praying together.

NOTES

HOLY AROMA

Sometimes the only way to get perspective on your life is to step outside it and look in.

Get hold of a digital camera and take photos of all the details of your day – the people you meet, the place you work, the places you eat, how you travel etc. In the evening, share your day with those who don't normally get to share it. Let them ask questions and make suggestions about your life.

Have you ever thought about the fact that there are some things photos just can't convey? Sound is one. Smell is another. It's just like looking into our lives without seeing the crucial missing aspect hovering in each photo – God's Spirit.

Read **2 Corinthians 2:14-17**.

With this passage as a basis, use the photos as a reminder to pray for all the relationships represented in them. Pray that you will be 'the aroma of Christ among those who are being saved and those who are perishing' even if this aroma is invisible to the naked eye. If you are a perfume or after shave user, then this could be a really useful daily prayer as you dab those fragrant drops on your neck, wrists or wherever.

You could meditate on this part of the verse

'God, through us, spreads everywhere the fragrance of the knowledge of him.'

What a thought, what a privilege and what a responsibility.

And you never know, your photo diary could end up as a piece of modern art in the Tate Modern. Or not.

NOTES

19

SERVICE THE CAR

John 13:1-17

Read this amazing passage slowly. Let Jesus ask you the question of verse 12 – **'Do you understand what I have done for you?'**

Walking was the main mode of transport in Jesus' time. In twenty-first century UK it is the car. That's why the place to meditate on that question and put these verses into practice is while washing a friend's or neighbour's car. (It's best to ask them about this first, or do it while you're doing your own.) This will give you the time and context for Jesus' attitude of service to take deeper root. If your first thought is 'I couldn't do that' or 'That would be humiliating' then cast your thoughts straight back to Jesus and ponder how the perfect Creator of all the universe must have felt; stooping to wipe the dust and grime from the feet of mere mortals, including the one who was about to betray him. As you struggle to remove the caked-on grime from the wing of the car, imagine what it must have been like to have the 'hands that flung stars into space' dare to touch the sweatiest, dirtiest part of the human body. Do we simply take ourselves too seriously and not take God seriously enough? What stops us getting on our knees to serve? As Jesus says, 'You should do I as I have done for you.'

Keep your eyes open for other simple acts of service that will genuinely help other people. If they are hard to see, then simply think about what help you could really do with to make your life easier, and the chances are that other people will be in the same boat.

Pray that something of the servant attitude of Jesus could be planted in you.

Philippians 2:6-8

> Who, being in very nature God,
>> did not consider equality with God something to be grasped,
> but made himself nothing,
>> taking the very nature of a servant,
>> being made in human likeness.
> And being found in appearance as a man,
>> he humbled himself
>> and became obedient to death—even death on a cross.

NOTES

20

GRACEFULLY RECEIVED

To begin with, make a list of your gifts and talents. If you need some help, you could phone a friend, as the chances are they may spot them more readily than you. You may also want to refer to the lists of gifts in Romans 12:6-8 or 1 Corinthians 12. Now rate each of these gifts/talents on a scale of 0 to 10, not based on the 'quality' of your giftings but on how much you are using them at this point in your life.

This exercise surprised me. There was so much of me that I was ignoring. Bring each of these areas to God in prayer, and together work on a strategy for increasing the use of your underused rusty giftings and talents. Like the old Fiesta that sits outside my house, the longer you leave something unused, the harder it is to restart.

Holding your giftings so close that they get mixed up in your own insecurities is a danger here, as opposed to holding them lightly as a gift. Holding gifts too close leads to a classic reaction when someone compliments you in regard to their use. Some folks will quickly reject the compliment; stating that 'Actually, it wasn't that great', point out all the mistakes they made, or say something like 'it's not me, it's God.' Your gifts have been given to you by God, so I think he cries when we don't enjoy the fact that we have them. It would be like Santa Claus overhearing us in conversation with our friends on Boxing Day saying 'Nah, the bike isn't that great really – you see the brakes squeak a bit, and I'm just not sure about the colour.' It is so easy to indulge in false humility, subconsciously seeking further affirmation. I have learnt that often the simple right response in these situations is to say 'Thank you.'

Were there spiritual gifts in those biblical lists that you desire? Be honest and ask God for them.

Matthew 7:11
> If you, then, though you are evil, know how to give good gifts to your children, how much more will your Father in heaven give good gifts to those who ask him.

NOTES ●❖

CURRENT A-PRAYERS

Romans 8:26

> In the same way, the Spirit helps us in our weakness. We do not know what we ought to pray for, but the Spirit himself intercedes for us with groans that words cannot express.

Watch the news on TV with two other people. Pray aloud during the news for the situations mentioned. Just let it be conversational. The false split between speaking to humans and speaking to God is often a major obstacle to our prayer lives developing. There is nothing wrong with alternately speaking to each other and God. I think he enjoys being part of a real conversation.

Be prepared to listen out for God's heart on various issues. Sometimes it will be anger, sometimes tears and sometimes celebration. Be encouraged that in those situations that seem too 'far gone', where hope is a distant memory, and we don't know what to pray for, that the Spirit is present literally making up the gap between the spiritual and the physical with groaning.

How often do we believe that being able to pray long articulate prayers is a sign of being 'spiritual'? If you took a definition of 'spiritual' as being 'like the Spirit', then being 'spiritual' is probably more accurately conveyed by someone feeling God's heart in their guts and simply groaning and crying, with few words. He wants our hearts more than he wants impressive grammar.

Attempt to develop trusting, interceding relationships with people, where you never have to impress each other with long sentences, but which provide the freedom to listen for and share God's heart.

We sometimes leave this sort of activity up to 'the intercessors', but there is no specific 'gift of intercession' or a group of people called 'intercessors' mentioned in my Bible. This is something we are all called to.

NOTES

BORN FREE

Luke 18:15-17

Today spend at least half an hour in your nearest big toy store. While wandering around, ask God to reconnect you with the values of innocence, joy and play that you once knew as a child. Often we sacrifice our childlikeness in a vain attempt to stop our childishness. Observe the other children in the store, and spot their freedom and carefree attitudes. (You may have to ignore the rampant commercialism and the parental realisation that this is a place of manipulation to be able to enjoy it.)

It may help to use these five words as 'headlines' to lead your thinking and praying. They mark out how a child interacts. Do these words describe your relationship with God?

- Honesty– tears, and squeals of laughter.
- Focus – distractions are thrown out of the way.
- Exuberance – even in just being me and moving my body.
- Inclusion – not checking your theology before playing with you.
- Spontaneity – unpredictable and sometimes beautiful.

As you pass out through the checkout, pray that out in the 'real world', you would not lose the sense of innocence and playfulness of a child. Pray for protection against the cynicism and world-weariness of adulthood.

SHINY HAPPY PEOPLE

Go into a large newsagents and flick through the magazines that you are instantly drawn to. Be honest. Go with your first gut reaction. I always believe that this exercise acts as a useful barometer of where our true interests lie, and also the areas in which we are most prone to having unhealthy idols. For me it is cricket and news magazines, and there's always the added problem of keeping my eyes on those, while much bare flesh is hovering close by.

Think back to Moses and the children of Israel in Exodus 32. While he was up Mount Sinai communing with God, they were down below getting restless, needing something to get excited about that would hold their attention. Aaron is desperate to keep this rebellious community together, so at the time the golden calf probably seemed like a good idea; bringing some focus and calming the masses. It was not an accident that idols were made of gold and carefully crafted. They had that 'wow' factor that grabbed the attention. Similarly our gaze is easily drawn by the airbrushed dazzle of "the bold and the beautiful" on magazine covers. The idol of celebrity, be that for the purposes of gossip or lust, has become incredibly shiny. Are we simply getting bored at the bottom of the mountain, finding a shiny but sub-standard and short-term channel for our enthusiasm? We are still attracted to things that are 'shiny', whether it be the Friends TV show, showbiz gossip or the latest worship leader. Should we be waiting on God, rather than filling our eyes and ears with non-God?

As you stand there, ask that God would start to reveal anything or anyone that has become an idol in your life.

Read **Acts 17:15-34**.

Madame Tussaud's got it just about right when they put Posh and Becks in their Nativity scene. Celebrity has become our spirituality and our aspiration. As with Aaron's situation, idols are cleverly never too obviously damaging – there is some purpose and good attached to them but they deflect our attention from where it should be placed.

Would the Apostle Paul walk into a newsagent or flick through satellite TV channels and be 'greatly distressed'? Are we? Or do we just accept it all as a fact of life?

Pray that God would dethrone any idols that have been revealed to you today. Name them and let a close friend know about it, so they can ask you how you're doing in the future.

PART 2

SEASON 1

NOTES●◆

ADDRESSES IN PENCIL

As I write, one of my best mates and his wife are moving house. The last few weeks have been challenging for them. There have been many logistical hassles and those silly little problems that you don't find out about until you actually move house. They have been finding out why moving house is up there with divorce and the loss of a loved one as one of the top three 'stressors' in people's lives. So when it's hard to countenance a move of just two miles with a big van and some burly men to help, how much harder was it to countenance moving hundreds of miles for a seventy-five year old man with the horde of relatives, animals and possessions he had accrued in his long life?

Read **Genesis 11:27-12:7**.

When you realise the logistics involved in Abram's potential house move, his obedience is all the more impressive. Just look at everything he is leaving behind. In verse 1 God commands him to 'Leave your country, your people and your father's household.' These three things would have been the bedrock of Abram's identity, safety and status, never mind his simple human need for friendship.

Are you living in the right place? Is your presence in your current location merely due to habit, comfort, security, fear of change, or do you actually feel called to be there? Would you have ears to hear if God called you to leave some of the people and places that make you feel loved, valued and safe? Recently many of my friends' lives have been in geographical flux, but a constant in all of their stories is that God blessed their socks off once they reached the place he was calling them to. In some cases it took large 'steps of faith' into the unknown, before the path became clear.

Take some time to pray about your 'geography'. If it has previously been a 'non-negotiable' with God, open it up for consideration now. The result may well be that the status quo remains, but you never know. You may want to use a map of the world, an A to Z, or a road atlas as an aid to your prayers.

Pete Greig famously said of a new generation of disciples that they 'write their addresses in pencil.'

Do you need a rubber?

NOTES

25

STAR SEARCH

For obvious reasons, this experience is slightly more powerful at night.

Pack warm clothes, a Bible and a torch. If you live in the city, get out of it, far enough to lose the light pollution, and spend at least twenty minutes just letting your eyes get accustomed to the wonder that is the night sky. During that time, you will begin to see more and more of what is there to be seen.

The nearest star you can see is four light years away, so you're seeing it as it was four years ago, and the furthest is 600,000 light years away, so you're seeing it as it was 600,000 years ago. So not only are you staring at a massive span of geography, you are staring up at a massive span of history, including snapshots from four years ago back to 600,000 years ago and everything in between (depending on your theology of creation). It blows my mind that I, as a puny little human being am allowed to experience that.

Spend some time simply giving thanks for what you see and what you are experiencing. Then read aloud the following passages, pausing to worship for some time after each one.

Psalm 147:4
> He determines the number of the stars
> and calls them each by name.

Job 22:12
> Is not God in the heights of heaven?
> And see how lofty are the highest stars.

Psalm 8

Philippians 2:14-16

Deuteronomy 4:19

> And when you look up to the sky and see the sun, the moon and the stars—all the heavenly array—do not be enticed into bowing down to them and worshipping things the Lord your God has apportioned to all the nations under heaven.

Someone once put it in song like this...

> I hear the song you wrote.
> I see the stars.
> They've waited years to quote
> Your words of power.

It may be a while since you last 'stood in awe' of God and his Creation, so allow yourself to be amazed at how someone so small could be so loved.

If you really can't get outside, then check out the website for a beautiful presentation of images from the Hubble telescope.

NOTES

EVERYBODY NEEDS SOMEBODY

Read **Genesis 2:15-18.**

In the book Bono on Bono,[4] there is a great quote from the man himself that says **'weakness drives us to friendships'**. Stop and think about that for a second. It pops up as he discusses how his lack of detailed musical knowledge means that he sometimes needs 'The Edge' to paint the chords around a melody. Bono, however, is the stronger at dreaming up melodies from scratch. Together they make an amazing team, as their multi-million album sales testify, filling the gaps in each others skill sets. Weakness drives them to friendship. It got me thinking that perhaps this is why we need friends.

Then my friend Lucy pointed out that God noted man's loneliness before the fall ('The Lord God said, "It is not good for the man to be alone. I will make a helper suitable for him" [Gen. 2:18]) suggesting that it is not simply our weaknesses that drive us to need friendship, somehow patching each other's holes, but a God-given need for others to share life with. It's the way he intended life to be.

My further thought, on reflection was that perhaps weakness is actually part of perfection. I'll leave you to wrestle with that one.

Who are you happy to admit that you need in your life? We often struggle to admit this in our desire to be self-sufficient. It is not failure to need people. It is human. No man is an island, it has been said. So why do we spend so much time chopping down the bridges that people build towards us? Ultimate success in this society is perceived as having your own car, your own house, your own wide-screen TV etc., as this gives you the maximum amount of control possible. If you live on your own, would it really be healthier for you to be living with someone else, even if it meant sacrificing some 'freedom'? Solo living (which is still possible to sneakily do in the midst of something that looks like community) almost inevitably breeds selfishness, and tunnel vision.

Spend some time in prayer thanking God for those people who you 'need' in your life, and ask God to re-orientate your life away from self-sufficiency. Can you think of any way that you and your friends could enshrine the truth that 'it is not good for man to be alone' in the way you organise your schedules and activities? What about a communal meal once a week? What about intentionally moving to the same area as each other? What about some shared sport instead of the solo run or gym session?

At this point, could you now tell your friends that you need them?

 NOTES

TURN AROUND

Walk around a park (or any large area) via a circular route (lakes are good for this). Take in everything there is to see. Even if you are limited to circling your house, still do it.

Then turn around. Walk in the opposite direction. You may be amazed at how different the same place can look. You may notice buildings that weren't so obvious, the different emphases of colour, the changed backdrop of the sky, and the change in shadows.

Now read **Acts 3:17-20**. Your experience underlines the 'turning around' that is repentance. It is more than simply saying sorry. It is a new way of seeing the same life. In which of your life situations do you need to not just say sorry to God, but walk through them in a completely different direction?

If you struggle to truly 'turn around' in various situations, then join the club. Often our spiritual instincts aren't dissimilar to our physical instincts, and I see my reticence to 'turning around' most when I'm trying to navigate towards a destination. After missing a turning, I will stubbornly keep trying to find another way that is 'just as quick' rather than swallow my pride and head back in the opposite direction. It's about being honest and admitting mistakes, rather than trying to 'fix' things ourselves.

Ask God to show you what your 'new direction' will look like in various situations. It may mean not going near the TV late at night. It may mean not going near high street clothes stores. Whichever direction it is, enjoy the new view.

NOTES

ON THE BRIGHT SIDE

I was sitting waiting for my sister one day in Northern Ireland. I was parked in full view of these beautiful rolling fields stretching back up a mountainside. However I was confused as to why the farmer had planted two different shades of grass. Some areas were bright green and some were dark green. I became even more confused when the different areas began moving. My fears of temporary insanity were relieved when I finally realised that it was the clouds that were moving overhead. D'oh!

My imagination continued to run however, as I could see myself as a little ant jumping around on the grass, always making sure I was in the bright green area. As soon as the shadow began to encroach, I would hop off to another bright section. God was speaking to me about my life. I was going out of my way to make sure that I was spending time where it was bright – i.e. where the popular people hung out, where I felt comfortable, where exciting things were happening, where things were going well. As soon as things became a bit awkward, I would ship off to find some excitement or comfort elsewhere. 'Am I called to that?' I thought, or am I called to stand still – to stand with people in their bright times and in their dark times, to share their joys and their sufferings?

You see our brains have developed 'suffering-avoidance' mechanisms that kick in when we see even a hint of effort coming around the corner. But when we intentionally remove ourselves from hard places, by choosing to live in a certain area of town, or a certain country, or choosing only 'safe' friends, we are limiting our discipleship, as well as the impact that we could be having on a hurting world. Read **Philippians 3:10,11**. Christ suffered, so to fully know Christ we must know what it is to suffer.

So today, instead of making excuses to leave a conversation that is beginning to bore you, inquire further about someone's life. Instead of saving pence by buying the cheapest groceries, buy some fairly traded produce. Instead of watching two soap operas, pray for four friends. These are only examples to get your mind working and I can't promise you will enjoy these options more, and you'd hardly define them as suffering, but you'll start to understand more about how your brain kicks in to limit your experience and discipleship.

Find a spot where you can sit and watch the impact of clouds moving across the sun. Spend some time asking God to show you which shadows you intentionally avoid, and where he might call you to sacrifice comfort for growth.

NOTES

29

STOP

Choose a place that you normally walk past, but instead stop there for fifteen minutes. Be still and simply turn on your senses. The author Ken Gire calls this discipline spotting 'windows of the soul'. Ask God to reveal things to you about his creation and his character from what you see, touch, taste, smell, and hear. Only when we stop for long enough to examine life in all its fullness, can we actually appreciate it, and worship the hands that are pulling the strings.

I'll never forget taking about twenty Youth For Christ volunteers to two separate fixed points; one looking down over a valley, and one in the centre of a town. They came back and shared many, many insights that God had given them during the fifteen minutes in both places. Every single one of them was different. Everyone reported how strange but refreshing it felt to just drink in God's world.

When I do this, I always notice something for the first time. It is always something that I would never have noticed if I had kept moving. The sheer volume of cars that pass a given point in five minutes. The stress on people's faces. The large number of text messages that are continually being bounced back and forth in a shopping centre. The subtle differences in the shape of a tree's leaves. The purity of the sun. The fact that no building no matter how high, even gets close to the sky. The tiny little insects whose names I will never know. The variety of colours available to an artist. I could go on, but the world is yours to discover and love. There is such complexity and such beauty combined with so much pain. Let's stop for long enough to take it in.

NOTES

PART 2

SEASON 1

30

PARTICIPATE IN THE DEBATE

Matthew 5:13-16

Salt can't preserve meat if stays in the salt-shaker. There is a reason street-lights aren't level with your knees. Sometimes what we do for God has to be public. As Christians, often our lack of engagement in politics is because we see it as corrupt, or too frightening a world to step into. Guess what? It is full of normal people who also previously thought that. But for some of us our reason for not engaging is because we don't honestly know which party we should join, and our indecision prevents us getting involved at all.

Today, visit the website www.politicalcompass.com, which asks you a series of issues-based questions, then places you on the political spectrum. You may be surprised at where you end up. You will see if you're sharing territory with Gordon Brown, George Bush, or Karl Marx. Sometimes only when we are provoked to answer a specific question do we realise, or start to articulate what our opinions are.

Whether you get involved with a party or not, as Christians we need to sharpen each other, so that when we are called to speak truth into a political issue, we can be articulate communicators, aware of the arguments, rather than ranting megaphones without the capacity to listen. You see the majority of councillors and MPs, despite their media portrayal, are servants of their communities – listening to them and acting on their behalf. There are many Christian MPs working hard for their constituents and the Kingdom at Westminster. It is very challenging, but when you speak to them you realise what a massive impact they are able to have on a wide range of issues, from fire extinguishers in Finchley, to international terrorism.

Is it time to roll up your sleeves?

You can find details about getting involved with your local branch of any of the main parties by visiting their websites –
www.labour.org.uk
www.conservatives.com
www.libdems.org.uk
www.greenparty.org.uk

 NOTES

SEASON 1

PART 3: ECCLESIASTES

31

CIRCLE OF LIFE

Take a deep breath, then read **Ecclesiastes Chapter 1**.

The writer of Ecclesiastes, Qoheleth, nicknamed 'the professor', uses the phrase **'under the sun'** in verse 3 and no less than thirty times in the whole book. He is unashamedly naming the place where his and our perspective comes from. After convincing and worrying us for a while (such as in verse 2), the writer eventually shows us that this 'ground-up' perspective is not all-encompassing. So often we extrapolate a moment from our lives to give it universal significance, but the truth is that eternal perspective can only be gained by one looking in from outside. The whole book has to be seen in this context.

Shrinking everything down to the trivial is best expressed by a simple expression – the shrug. You could describe Ecclesiastes as the world's oldest and longest shrug, whose purpose is to scare us into believing that the shruggers have got it right. It is a skilful deconstruction of our world-view, intentionally pulling us apart to put us back together in a shape that will cope with the randomness of life.

When verse 8 states that, 'All things are wearisome, more than one can say.', it has strangely familiar ring. 'Whateverrr.' 'Am I boverred?' Nothing seems to matter and nothing seems to impress us any more. It's as if the Christmas TV schedule has become a metaphor for all of life – 'What has been will be again, what has been done will be done again; there is nothing new under the sun' (verse 9). Our senses are fed and fed, but never filled. As verse 8 says, 'the eye never has enough of seeing, nor the ear its fill of hearing.'

There is a circular nature to life. Many good things done are quickly undone. History continually shows the ebb and flow of justice and injustice. Hopes are raised, then dashed. We hope that some day we will learn, but more people were killed in the twentieth century than all the others put together.

Make a list of all the activities, noble or otherwise, with conscious or subconscious motivations, with which you seek to bring meaning, pleasure and significance to your life. You could look at your actions on one particular day, or you could use the writer's list as a template for your own (it's pretty extensive). It is important to play devil's advocate as the writer of Ecclesiastes is doing. Was there any point to any of it? In the big scheme of things what did you achieve? How did it benefit the human race? Will it last beyond your death? Beyond the death of this earth? When you break our activities down, it is very easy to come to the conclusion that many of them are in fact meaningless.

Read back through your list, and after every item write or say, 'Yet it is meaningless'.

But are they all meaningless? Grapple with the question.

No happy ending today. That's the whole point of Ecclesiastes. It's designed to leave us crying, 'No but yeah, but no, but yeah, but....'

NOTES

32

PLEASURE-SEEKER

Take yourself to your favourite spot in your area, be that a coffee shop, a park or a library. Go to a place that makes you feel good.

If anyone could find satisfaction, this writer could. He establishes his credentials early in the piece. Read **Ecclesiastes 2:1-11**.

I really wish that folks could read this chapter before wasting their time finding out for themselves. Some people spend a whole life working their way through all the possibilities that might actually bring meaning to life. Helpfully the writer has crossed those bridges already. His life is not without some thought. Note that he develops from mere hedonism to seeking meaning in creativity and production. Not ignoble, you may think. But still meaningless. He says it was 'like chasing the wind'. Now read this potent story.

An American businessman was at a pier in a small coastal Mexican village when a small boat with just one fisherman docked. Inside the small boat were several large yellow-fin tuna. The American complimented the Mexican on the quality of his fish and asked how long it took to catch them.

The Mexican replied only a little while.

The American then asked why didn't he stay out longer and catch more fish.

The Mexican said he had enough to support his family's immediate needs.

The American then asked the Mexican how he spent the rest of his time.

The Mexican fisherman said, 'I sleep late, fish a little, play with my children, take siesta with my wife, Maria, stroll into the village each evening where I sip wine and play guitar with my amigos. I have a full and busy life, señor.'

The American scoffed, 'I am a Harvard MBA and could help you. You should spend more time fishing and, with the proceeds, buy a bigger boat. With the proceeds from the bigger boat, you could buy several boats, eventually you would have a fleet of fishing boats. Instead of selling your catch to a middleman you would sell directly to the processor, eventually opening your own cannery. You would control the product, processing and distribution.'

'You would need to leave this small coastal fishing village and move to Mexico City, then LA and eventually New York where you will run your expanding enterprise.'

The Mexican fisherman asked, 'But señor, how long will this all take?'

To which the American replied, 'Fifteen to twenty years.'

'But what then, señor?' asked the Mexican.

The American laughed, and said, 'That's the best part. When the time is right, you would announce an IPO and sell your company stock to the public. You'll become very rich, you would make millions!'

'Millions, señor?' replied the Mexican. 'Then what?'

The American said, 'Then you would retire. Move to a small coastal fishing village where you would sleep late, fish a little, play with your kids, take a siesta with your wife, stroll to the village in the evenings where you could sip wine and play your guitar with your amigos.'

On hearing this story, I knew I'd heard it somewhere before – Ecclesiastes 2:24-25

> A man can do nothing better than to eat and drink and find satisfaction in his work. This too, I see, is from the hand of God, for without him, who can eat or find enjoyment?

Do we try to get to a place of 'satisfaction' in our lives, or do we try to find satisfaction in the midst of our lives? There is a subtle, but massive difference. Answer the question honestly by writing the story of your life as you would like to see it develop from this point onward. You have five hundred words to dream for yourself.

NOTES

33

TIMEWARP

Read **Ecclesiastes chapter 3**.

There is one week of my school experience that I will never forget. A lovely young guy called Philip Johnston was killed in a bicycle accident. For many of the pupils, it was our first encounter with the frailty of life. The headmaster wisely allowed us all to go to the funeral, and you could feel five hundred young heads and hearts trying to process this strange new information.

Later that week, we were scheduled to perform a concert for many of the local pensioners. There was a strong accent on comedy, and a group of us were performing 'Summer Nights' from Grease, with a twist – the girls were in leather jackets and denim, and the boys were in...well you get the picture. In light of the recent events, it all felt a bit strange, and we wondered about not going ahead with the routine. However we did go ahead, and as ever the old folks loved it.

A few days later I was wandering around the imposing cathedral of St. Patrick in Armagh, and there was a massive Bible sitting open at Ecclesiastes chapter 3. The words jumped out at me –

> a time to weep and a time to laugh,
> a time to mourn and a time to dance.

Something of the reality of life was planted in me that week, and more importantly, the truth that God knew and understood. Reading those verses it was as if I heard him saying 'I know, I know. But it won't always be this way.'

Which of the statements in the passage most resonate with you?

Are there specific periods of your life that you could reference to some of the phrases?

Write a paragraph about those times, exploring how you felt, and why. But also write some notes about that phrase's 'opposite'.

There is a rhythm here, that speaks of the changing seasons of life. Whoever promised us that we would live in eternal summer? Thank God for the varying seasons of your life.

NOTES

DIVINE DISCONTENT

Ecclesiastes 3:9-14

The highpoint of this passage is verse 11 –

> He has made everything beautiful in its time. He has also set eternity in the hearts of men; yet they cannot fathom what God has done from beginning to end.

This eternity in our hearts helps to explain some of the frustrations we have with the state of the earth for we know it simply doesn't compare with what is ticking away inside us. But we try to suppress it, because sometimes it's just too painful. What we ourselves are faced with, or what we see in the wider world just seems too far from that eternal perfection, so it's easier to ignore it. A sense of eternity is what enables us to cry with Jesus for the broken and the hungry. It is what enables us to get angry about injustice. Something in us screams the truth of eternity, yet as the rest of verse 11 reveals, we cannot totally 'fathom' God. If we could, we would be on a level with him or above him, and I can't speak for everyone, but quite frankly, I'm not. Today, officially accept your citizenship of eternity.

Now draw a time line on a roll of paper around the walls of a room to represent your life. Place points up to 100% above the x-axis representing positive moments, and points to 100% below the x-axis representing negative moments, as the years have ticked by. Estimate what it will look like for the rest of your days on earth, and then continue it around the rest of the walls, as a reminder that life extends beyond this mortal body with its ups and downs to become one long eternal 100% plateau.

Ecclesiastes 3:14

I know that everything God does will endure for ever; nothing can be added to it and nothing taken from it. God does it so that men will revere him.

Eternity has been defined as 'the period beyond the present' – What a fantastic definition. Stop and take it in for a second. Eternity is everything after now. Whoops, here it is again. Do you feel like you're part of eternity? You are.

Look back at the events of your week. What moments do you think had eternal significance, rather than significance only for this life? Give thanks for them, and pray for more.

NOTES●◆

35

OPPRESSED ON ALL SIDES

Some would say these are some of the saddest verses in the Bible:

Ecclesiastes 4:1-3

> Again I looked and saw all the oppression that was taking place under
> the sun:
> I saw the tears of the oppressed—
> and they have no comforter;
> power was on the side of their oppressors—
> and they have no comforter.
> And I declared that the dead,
> who had already died,
> are happier than the living,
> who are still alive.
> But better than both
> is he who has not yet been,
> who has not seen the evil
> that is done under the sun.

The reality of these verses came home to me on the 19th May 2004. I remember the date because it was the day that my beautiful niece Hannah was born. I was anxiously waiting for news from the hospital, as it had been a far from simple labour. To kill time, I flicked through various TV news channels and I couldn't believe my eyes. In the space of just one hour, an Iraqi wedding near the Syrian border was bombed (killing around forty people), a march in Gaza was bombed (killing about the same number), Tony Blair was hit by a condom full of purple paint during Prime Minister's questions, Rudy Guiliani was being heckled by 9/11 victims' families at the 9/11 inquest and American generals were trying to explain what had happened at Abu Ghraib to a Senate committee. I thought – 'What kind of world are we welcoming you into, my little one? I am so sorry that we couldn't get things better tidied up for your arrival. I would fully understand if you never wanted to come out.'

The tears that I saw that day are merely a drop in the ocean of the 'tears of the oppressed' all over this planet. There are many people and organisations who are trying to comfort the oppressed today, but there are many more that still have 'no comforter'. Pray about what 'comforting' role God may call you into. It may be physically in another country, or it may be by giving financially to an organisation like Tearfund. Visit their website today – www.tearfund.org

Sometimes the only way to help the oppressed is to confront their oppressor. Check out the work of the International Justice Mission, who physically remove those caught up in forced and bonded labour all over the world, especially those being used as sex slaves: www.ijm.org

Derek Kidner in his book on Ecclesiastes[5] closes with these sobering words 'While we, as Christians, see further than he (the author) allowed himself to look, it is no reason to spare ourselves the realities of the present.'

NOTES

36

COMPETITION TIME

Today's devotion is a competition. The winner will be the first user to email the website with the longest verse in the Bible and as a prize will receive a £100 book token. Try it now.

Ecclesiastes 4:4

And I saw that all labour and all achievement spring from man's envy of his neighbour. This too is meaningless, a chasing after the wind.

Did you feel how much a competition gets us going? Even those of us who claim that 'we're not competitive' still have that human sense of 'survival of the fittest' running through us. The truth is that the most dangerous competitiveness is not the obvious physical competitiveness exhibited by many people during sport and board games. It is the slowly smouldering competitiveness that makes us desire a better car, better house, better clothes, or closer relationship with the church leader than our fellow members. You may say, 'Oh, that's nothing to do with being competitive – We just want something better.' To which I ask the question 'Why?' The cult of comparison often springs from our own insecurities about our intelligence, our looks, or our popularity. Would we desire to move to the next level if nobody else was there? Why as we get older have many of our cars become shinier and snazzier? Would we buy fashionable clothes if no-one else was? We'd like to think so, but is that really true? What makes them fashionable? Why do we think we need such big TVs and so many channels? Why do we need so much stuff?

Be brutally honest. What of your neighbours' lifestyle do you envy? What items or activities secretly feed your subconscious desire to keep up? There is no point in pretending we don't have it. It is in our DNA. Pray that God would illuminate the areas where this manifests itself in our lives, and mould us to be more like the Son of Man, who had 'nowhere to lay his head', and didn't seem remotely concerned about it.

Insert a little reminder card into wherever you keep your money; be that wallet or handbag or pocket. Scribble just one word on it. As you spend longer hours at work, or spend excessive money, let it remind you of one question – 'Why?'

NOTES ●◆

37

AIR-CONDITIONING

Ecclesiastes 4:6

Better one handful with tranquillity
than two handfuls with toil
and chasing after the wind.

The first phrase of this verse has also been translated **'a handful of quietness'**.
What a beautiful thought. How often do I need to drop my 'handfuls of toil'
and pick up a handful of quietness. Using your body as a physical prayer, drop
whatever stresses and strains you are gripping onto, and just grab a big dollop
of quiet air into your hand. Hold it for ten minutes. Ask God to bring you a
contentment that your own hands will never be able to.

Ecclesiastes 4:8

There was a man all alone;
he had neither son nor brother.
There was no end to his toil,
yet his eyes were not content with his wealth.
"For whom am I toiling," he asked,
"and why am I depriving myself of enjoyment?"
This too is meaningless —
a miserable business.

It's hard to believe the writer has not spent time in New York, or the city of
London. It's hard to believe he has not been interviewing the ex-husbands
and ex-wives of those whose jobs have become all-consuming. It is a solemn
warning to us all. Print or write this verse on a card and put it above your
desk, or place of work.

NOTES

NOTHING NEW UNDER THE SUN

Ecclesiastes 5:8-10

> If you see the poor oppressed in a district, and justice and rights denied, do not be surprised at such things; for one official is eyed by a higher one, and over them both are others higher still. The increase from the land is taken by all; the king himself profits from the fields. Whoever loves money never has money enough; whoever loves wealth is never satisfied with his income. This too is meaningless.

We shouldn't be surprised by institutional sin amongst multinational corporations or governments when we read these verses from thousands of years previous. Often our energies are focused on helping those at the receiving end of injustice, which is good and right, but perhaps we should be focusing more attention on the injustice itself. In Rich Christians in an Age of Hunger,[6] Ron Sider describes an interesting test. There is a tap filling a bucket of water in front of you. Your task is to stop the bucket overflowing, and you have a teaspoon in your hand. What do you do?

Sadly, many of our efforts to help the poor focus on frantically spooning water out of the bucket. You can help to cut off the tap at source by campaigning for a fairer world economic system, more controls on multinational corporations and greater democracy and accountability in international organisations like the WTO (World Trade Organisation) and the IMF (International Monetary Fund).

This is a quote from an editorial of The Economist w/b 2 Feb 2004

> The selfish pursuit of profit serves a social purpose. And this is putting it mildly. The standard of living people in the West enjoy today is due

to little else but the selfish pursuit of profit.... This is not the fatal defect of capitalism, it is the very reason capitalism works.

On one level they are right. Capitalism does work. But without some fundamental restructuring, it only works for the small percentage with capital at the top of the economic pile. If you've bought this book, you're one of those at the top of the pile. Half of the world's population lives on less than $2 a day. There is somebody somewhere suffering directly as a result of our comfort.

There is not enough space here to get into the detailed arguments of what needs to happen in terms of debt relief and creating a level playing field for developing countries to be able to trade their way forward, but the websites you can access from www.makepovertyhistory.org all provide fantastic information and resources for campaigning. Help turn off that tap.

Speak (www.speak.org.uk) are a wonderful organisation who combine campaigning and prayer. Their campaigns may be focused on national Governments, international bodies such as the IMF, or big business. Get involved.

Other recommended reading:
Globalisation and its discontents – Joseph Stiglitz
The End of Poverty – How we can make it happen in our lifetime –
Jeffrey Sachs, Penguin Books

NOTES ●◆

39

HISTORY HAS NO FAVOURITES

We need to change location for today's reading. **Go to the accident and emergency department of your local hospital.** This is a place of genuine apprehension for people. It is also a place of great 'levelling', in that there will be people waiting to be treated from every background, religion and age group. Take a seat.

Ecclesiastes 9:1-12

If our journey through Ecclesiastes is like a plane ride, you get a sense that in chapter 9, after all the turbulence of the early chapters, we are just beginning to level out, and our stomachs are just starting to return from the upper reaches of our chest cavities. We definitely haven't landed yet, however.

Somewhere deep down, we still believe that because we belong to God, we should expect a slightly easier passage through this life. There are a number of subtle influences that have fed this lie throughout our lives, resulting in a default 'gut feeling' that it is the case. This is even though there is next to no biblical foundation for such a way of thinking. I think what we experience is a form of 'projection'. It's what we'd like to think, and we therefore project our preferred world-view onto the truth of how things are. However there is a definite absence of such rose-tinted glasses in chapter 9. We are encountering bright white truth, even if hurts our eyes slightly.

In Matthew 5:45, either Jesus is doing an Ian McCaskill impression, and making a purely meteorological point, or he is adding his considerable weight to those words from Ecclesiastes, 'He causes his sun to rise on the evil and the good, and sends rain on the righteous and the unrighteous.'

This is the sort of thing that it is enormously helpful to sort out in our heads and hearts before the tough times appear, but even this provides no immunity. Some perspective helps, because if this line of thinking is true, then it could be regarded as a bit of a bum deal if this life was all that there is. But it's not. These seventy or eighty years are like the hours of painful labour, before the decades of joy. Spend some time praying for the other people in the waiting room, and ask God for the grace to react well to the 'trials' of our lives, so the next time we are in that waiting room (real or virtual) of apprehension, we can know that it's not a moment where God is absent.

James 1:2-4

> Consider it pure joy, my brothers, whenever you face trials of many kinds, because you know that the testing of your faith develops perseverance. Perseverance must finish its work so that you may be mature and complete, not lacking anything.

NOTES

ENDGAME

Ecclesiastes 12:11-14

So it turns out that perhaps everything isn't meaningless, after all. Judgement doesn't sound particularly meaningless. That sounds like something I want to understand. Our pretensions have been stripped away to leave only what matters.

Here is the dictionary definition of a 'goad' (v11)

1. A long stick with a pointed end used for prodding animals.
2. An agent or means of prodding or urging; a stimulus.

The depth of the imagery here is wonderful. God is our 'one Shepherd', who sometimes uses pointed statements (goads) from others to turn our heads, so that our bodies will move in a certain direction. It may not be pleasant, but we end up pointed the right way. How do you react to 'goading'? In these verses, there is also the sense of allowing wisdom to penetrate deeply into our minds like an embedded nail sinks deep into wood. Once nails like that go in, it is very hard to get them out.

Cast your mind back to twelve or so years ago. I'm sure at one time or another you experienced being in a car that was pulled over for speeding (obviously only as a passenger). In these circumstances there always seemed to be some 'wiggle room.' If the police officer discovered that you were a doctor on the way to a hospital, or the local mayor, or a businessman with connections, or just liked your smile, there was a chance that you might get off with a caution. This is, of course, no longer the case. We have our beloved speed cameras. (While we're on the subject, do you let God into your decisions about what speed to drive at?)

These days, it doesn't matter from what social class, gender, circumstance, race, or creed you are coming from. There is only one factor that will decide whether or not you are going to receive a friendly little letter in the post, and that is your speed. It strikes me that this is a amazing modern image for what is being discussed in verses 13 and 14. There are some rules that I stick to because I want to, but if I'm honest there are some rules that I stick to because I fear the consequences if I don't. When we are judged, our backgrounds and status will not matter. There is only one factor that will decide whether our names will appear in another important book, and that is our response to Jesus.

This is hopefully a helpful 'trigger thought'. I now can't drive past a speed camera without thinking about 'fearing God and keeping his commandments' (verse 13), knowing that he searches behind my actions to my motives, 'including every hidden thing, whether it is good or evil.' Get into the discipline of using such imagery as triggers for prayer, as shepherds, fishermen and farmers would have been able to in Jesus' time. Otherwise as humans we simply don't remember to remember, and the nails that could be firmly embedded in our minds simply bounce off our thick skulls. Keep your eyes open for many and varied 'trigger thoughts' like these. If it helps to lodge a thought in your mind, go out and take a picture of the object. If you're taking a photo of a speed camera, you have the added joy of the delicious irony.

NOTES●◆

SEASON 2

PART 1: LUKE

WAITING FOR THE NOD

Luke 1:5-20

We can perhaps forgive Zechariah for not grabbing the big picture straight away. After all, God has not spoken for four hundred years. This is quite an event. It is the end of 'the silence', and here he is, an ageing priest, right in the middle of it. There is also a huge paradigm shift taking place. This was the start of the Kingdom being at hand, in the flesh, rather than at a distance. Add to that the fact that a glowing angel is a few feet away from you, and all in all it's a lot to process for a first century BC man. In the midst of all this mental, spiritual and emotional turmoil the angel says, 'Do not be afraid, Zechariah; your prayer has been heard.'

My question to you is whether, in the midst of the flurry of your life, you can be as disorientated as Zechariah, and fail to notice that little phrase being whispered to you? Do you believe that your prayers have been heard? In so many life situations, what we really want is not necessarily someone to provide solutions (even though God does do that in this case) but simply someone to listen. Is our 'stream of consciousness' style of praying preventing us from hearing the 'Yeah... Ahuh...' or even the subtle nod of the head that lets us know we are being heard?

One of the phenomenons of the early twenty-first century is 'traffic calming', and Luton has plenty. One of my favourite road-signs is the one with a big black car, but a small red car, that tells you who has right of way in an artificially squeezed road. Does your prayer life ever feel like that? There's only room for movement in one direction, and it's from you to God. You drive on through, and only then has the still, small voice got space to move towards you, by which time you're gone. Maybe it's time to 'give way'.

Spend some time today praying to God, but leaving the space to listen, hear, know and rejoice in the fact that someone is listening, hearing and acting.

Draw a 'two-way traffic' sign and place it on your wall to remind you.

If that last suggestion made you think, 'I couldn't put that on the wall', then do have a think about how you use your environment creatively to help your spiritual life. We all need all the help we can get. Ignoring these things is like an asthmatic not taking their inhaler so they can 'learn to do without'. This is medical nonsense to rival our spiritual pride.

PART 1: LUKE

SEASON 2

NOTES●◆

42

THE BIG PICTURE

Take this devotion to a bus stop or train platform. Along with the other folks there, sit and wait.

Luke 1:21-25

God knows the big picture. He simply calls us to be obedient and play our part in the big story. Zechariah could not have known that his simple actions would pave the way for the salvation of mankind. In a world that is constantly looking for and congratulating numerical results, we need to be aware that our impact on just one person could change a generation. We never know in what chain we could be a vital link. Would it make a difference to how we look at certain relationships, if we knew what that person or their offspring, or a person that they influence, will go on to achieve? Jesus related to people like this. We are called to see the potential in people when others write them off.

Luke 1:23
   When his time of service was completed, he returned home.

So Zechariah has just had a life-changing, destiny-fulfilling experience. If that was me, I think I would be running home straight away with glee to tell the wife, 'Guess what is happening, and guess what we have to do!' Remember he has been praying for the deliverance of his people and for a child for years and years! The time of service referred to in the passage would have been a whole week, so Zechariah's dedication to his job is impressive. It is even more impressive bearing in mind that job satisfaction is often associated with the ability to speak.

Patiently waiting for God to do his thing is a difficult discipline. Read Isaiah 60. Some of the most majestic language in scripture is contained here. As you read it, you are crying out with excitement for these moments to come soon, when Jews and Gentiles will again be together in a glorious, prosperous Kingdom. Superlative after superlative is building the momentum up to a climax and then you hit the last verse.

Isaiah 60:22
> I am the Lord;
> in its time I will do this swiftly.

Do we start building our kingdoms at the first sign of excitement? Do we trust God's timing? As the verse from Isaiah shows, waiting for the Lord's timing means things happen easily, rather than with the trudge we sometimes experience from pushing on ahead. Can you keep a secret? Do you wait for the right opportunity before sharing information, at which time it may be more powerful? Have you been able to wait at the bus stop? Or have you moved on already?

NOTES

43

ASKING FOR TROUBLE

Luke 1:26-38

A quick note on Gabriel. He was no post-room messenger boy, simply delivering a memo. Earlier in verse 19, Gabriel stated that 'I am Gabriel. I stand in the presence of God.' The actual wording he uses here alludes to the eastern custom of a prime minister having access to his monarch at all times. He has the regular ear of God the Father, and though he does not hold ultimate sovereignty as a monarch does, Gabriel is stating his authority clearly. Given the importance of his messages to Zechariah, Mary and Joseph, it's not surprising that God sent his 'top man'.

Luke 1:35

> The angel answered, "The Holy Spirit will come upon you, and the power of the Most High will overshadow you. So the holy one to be born will be called the Son of God.

The miracle-working power that will 'overshadow' Mary here is the same power mentioned when the Holy Spirit is 'brooding over the waters' in Genesis 1:2. How fantastic is that? The same supernatural force that brought life and fertility from barrenness to the original creation brings fertility to a virgin's womb. Yet again, the big story holds together, as the Son of Man who will reconcile all creation to himself appears in its midst with both the essence of the Creator and the created in him.

What may God be attempting to birth in you? What creative spark may the Creator be placing in you? Have you allowed the Holy Spirit to 'brood over' or 'overshadow' you? As with Mary, if we let this process happen, it will require our obedience and willingness to suffer on his behalf.

Luke 1:38

> "I am the Lord's servant," Mary answered. "May it be to me as you have said."

In case we haven't got a handle on what Mary had to suffer to be obedient, think of her situation in these terms: in the conversation of your workplace, what situations define someone failing in life, whether implicitly or explicitly? Divorce, drugs, getting the sack? What news makes everyone look at their feet and go 'Well...ah...'? This is the sort of reaction that Mary would have known she would get when her pregnancy became obvious, yet she still said 'May it be to me as you have said.' Does God know if you are willing to endure hardship for the sake of his glory? Let him know if you are.

People talk about having the gift of hospitality, but I'm not so sure that we're not all meant to be hospitable. I recently enjoyed the most amazing hospitality at a retreat centre where the 'Sisters of Mary' went out of their way to provide food, rest and space. It was the little things that meant so much. They model their hospitality on Mary's willingness to be 'hospitable' to the Saviour in her very own body but, as with Mary, this hospitality has a cost to their own comfort. They lose their private space to those invading, as Mary did.

So exercise some hospitality. Plan to welcome some folks who are in need of a welcome. Pray that you would hold less dearly to your private space. When we let folks become part of our lives, we are often surprised by how much we receive from them, as we are giving to them.

So stop reading right now and fix up an invitation by phone or email. Anyone can do this. We have begun to confuse great catering with hospitality. The issue is togetherness, not the cuisine.

NOTES

KINDRED SPIRITS

Luke 1:39-42

> At that time Mary got ready and hurried to a town in the hill country of Judea, where she entered Zechariah's home and greeted Elizabeth. When Elizabeth heard Mary's greeting, the baby leaped in her womb, and Elizabeth was filled with the Holy Spirit. In a loud voice she exclaimed: 'Blessed are you among women, and blessed is the child you will bear.'

This is one of my favourite moments in Scripture. Mary has only to say hello, and Elizabeth knows immediately in her gut what is going on. There is mutual joy as the future hope that has been planted in both their bodies leaps skyward. Are there people who have similar passions, hopes and dreams to you? When you meet them, do you feel a 'leaping in your spirit'? Some call them 'kindred spirits' or 'brothers-in-arms'. Sometimes they are not even people you know very well, but when you see them 'do their thing', you feel this gut connection. My mate Tim is convinced that he and Jamie Oliver are made of the same stuff. I'm praying that they will meet up someday.

Life is too short to not share passions and encourage each other. Today, organise to spend some time with your kindred spirit so that you can do each other some good. Sometimes the people whom we feel understand us best live miles from us, so you could organise a 'skype' session (www.skype.com: free Internet phone call), or a weekend visit. There may be more members of your 'tribe' than you think. Check out websites and Internet forums on the subjects or issues you are passionate about. We all need to build faith into each other. Dreams are trampled so easily in today's world, so when we find people we understand, we need to cheer them on, as they may well feel that no-one else understands them. When you're with them one-on-one, pray that the dreams that he has planted in both of you will come 'to term' as those significant babies did.

Luke 1:45

> Blessed is she who has believed that what the Lord has said to her will be accomplished.

NOTES ●◆

45

MAKE THE LAST FIRST

Luke 1:51-53

> He has performed mighty deeds with his arm;
> He has scattered those who are proud in their inmost thoughts.
> He has brought down rulers from their thrones
> but has lifted up the humble.
> He has filled the hungry with good things
> but has sent the rich away empty.

Mary is rejoicing in the 'upside-down' world of the Kingdom of God.

We still live in a world where 'might is right' and the gap is still growing between rich and poor. In what ways are we seeking to turn the world upside-down? In what ways are we being counter-cultural? Do we challenge the colleague, boss or church leader who is using power to wield influence? Do we allow a team member to use their mood or threat of a mood to influence decision-making?

Somehow we are attracted to those who have most earthly power. We seem to believe that certain people might just do us a favour, or will sprinkle some 'magic dust' on us. You can see this at meetings where politicians are present. Everyone hovers around them, hoping for some power to rub off. But you can also see this in a playground, where people hover around the person with the most power. They may be the loudest, the cheekiest, the rudest, or the strongest. This isn't the way of things in God's Kingdom. In his Kingdom, the 'last shall be first' and the 'meek will inherit the earth', because they haven't grabbed it and controlled it.

Today resolve to strike a blow for the underdog. Stand up for the guy or girl who is normally the brunt of the office jokes. Make way in the queue for the mother struggling with her kids. Take time to chat to the ancillary staff in your building.

I heard the author Stuart Briscoe crystallise some of this Kingdom thinking recently. He said 'We express the Kingdom when we do what is good instead of what is comfortable, when we do what is right instead of what is profitable, and when we stand by what is true rather than what is popular.' Weigh up some of your recent decisions on these three axes, and see how you're doing. It may help to draw them out as shown (see illustration), and then plant your decisions on the line.

My mate Colin impresses me with his attitude to business. On meeting a new boss, he always tells them, 'I won't lie for you.' But he follows it with, 'And that's a good thing, because it means I won't lie to you, either.' That at least turns the property surveying part of this world upside-down.

NOTES

46

SWIMMING UPSTREAM

For a whole day, intentionally walk against the crowd. Whether that's going up the wrong side of the stairs, or coming out of the wrong exit, see how it feels to be going against the flow. (Obviously don't be intentionally rude.) I don't recommend extending this to driving in one-way streets. This discomfort is something we need to become accustomed to, because as Christians, I believe, we will have to swim against the prevailing tide increasingly in the years to come.

Luke 1:57-66

The crowd are astonished that Zechariah and Elizabeth are breaking with tradition, but nothing is going to change their decision, because they have both heard from God. Are we too easily swayed by the crowd and tradition? Is the path of least resistance the one we most often tread? Do we choose silence rather than letting our unpopular view be heard? There will be times in our lives when we are in a minority of one, but still right.

Ask God for the calm grace of Zechariah who didn't become antagonistic, but simply said 'His name is John.' Surprise people today with your points of view, but also surprise them by your grace in communicating them. Jesus never blurted from a defensive or insecure place. He spoke with calm authority. Pray for more of that in your life today. People know it when they see it.

It may help to make a list of areas where you feel that you are swimming against the tide. Next time you are with your small group, mention these situations so they can pray for you in them, and so you can receive reassurance that what you're standing up for is right and that you're not just being pig-headed, or going insane.

NOTES

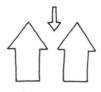

47

FAR FROM FANTASY

Luke 2:1-7

It's almost over before it's begun. There is no fanfare (the angels come next). You've finished reading before you realise what you've read. The most important moment in the history of the universe so far has just happened. God has become man.

Perhaps we have become so used to (as the Commercial Insurance ads used to say) 'making a drama (or nativity) out of a crisis' that we have lost track of some of the normality of Jesus' birth. There was no digital timer counting down in the corner of the screen, no electric light, no live webcam etc. This was a birth unlike any other, but actually strangely similar to every other. God entered history. Our history. He entered not some far-imagined fantasy land like Middle Earth, but the Middle East of our earth. Jesus was delivered into the reality of life on earth. My earth. Your earth.

As a mental exercise, trace your life back to the year of your birth. Stop off at the holidays, new jobs, and accidents as well as the obvious birthdays, weddings and funerals. It doesn't take long to get back to zero, does it? Where does the time go? You only have to extend that process a few more times and you're back there, knocking on a stable door. I'm just trying to underline the point that Jesus was part of our history, not that long ago. This is the reverse process to the opening titles of the Star Trek series, Enterprise, which goes out of its way to connect the dots to the near future, so we don't feel that the show is happening in a world different from ours.

So now return to the start of your life's journey. To the time and place you were born. If Jesus had instead been born at the same moment and in the same area that you were born, what would be different and what would be the same about his life? Where would he have gone to school? Who would he have hung out with? What job would he have done? What helpful comparisons could you make between this life and your own?

Craft your thoughts in the form of a story, using your experiences as a template.

NOTES

DARKER SKY, BRIGHTER STAR

It's worth dwelling on this momentous event for a little longer.

Is there an area or street in your town where house prices are lowest and people would laugh if you even mentioned that you were thinking of moving there? It may be run down, disused, seedy or simply 'the wrong end of town'. You know the sort of place I'm talking about. Go there to read today's passage.

Luke 2:1-12.

The divine nature is incredibly exposed in the fact that God chose the most obscure, private but degrading surroundings for the most beautiful moment of his union with humanity and the most public place in the capital city for his most degrading moment. How would you feel if your wedding took place in a car park? Or if your secret sins were exposed all over the tabloid press?

In what dark places do you not even bother to look for God working? Where are the 'stables' of your family, your town or your country? Take some time to think about this.

Because you can bet there is a divine presence right in the midst. Those Christians who work with and among the poor of the world know the truth that the Magi also discovered. You meet Jesus there. In his book Christianity Rediscovered,[7] Vincent Donovan talks extensively about our arrogant attitudes with regard to mission. He speaks of our belief that we somehow 'take God' to people, when actually he is already there and through our interaction we may hope to increase people's awareness of him at work, including our own.

Pray that God would give you some sort of 'bright star' to lead you to these places.

Now walk up and down the street or place where you read the passage, and pray for this place and its inhabitants, asking that they would know the God who is at work amongst them.

NOTES

49

TREASURED TIMES

Luke 2:15-20

Luke 2:19
> But Mary treasured up all these things and pondered them in her heart.

Now I know that neither you nor I (definitely not me) will ever experience the privilege of giving birth to the Saviour of the world, but we have something significant to learn from Mary here. Do we treasure up our experiences? Do you keep a journal or take note of the randomness of your life? I often regret not having done this more conscientiously during mine. This is not mere factual recall. This is 'treasuring' – there is value and affection attached to these memories. 'Cherish' is a rare word in our instant culture. To spend time cherishing an experience would mean that we are wasting the time that we could be using to experience another experience. The word for 'pondered' here literally means 'to weigh'. Mary was balancing these experiences against what she believed to be true about her Son.

Take some time to scribble on separate postcards certain life experiences and keep them in an envelope as 'treasure'. Cherish them. Weigh up what they teach you about your life and mission here on earth.

Add extra postcards to the envelope as further events occur in your life.

NOTES

50

WHAT ARE YOU WAITING FOR?

Luke 2:21-32

This is one of the most beautiful stories I have ever read. Read it again, attempting to get inside the mind and heart of this old man at the end of his time on earth. Try to feel what he is feeling. Has there been a situation in your life where a moment of amazing joy made all the waiting worthwhile?

What are you waiting for? Simeon was 'moved' (v27) by God's Spirit because he was 'waiting for the consolation of Israel' (v25). Are you waiting for the coming Kingdom? Are you expecting it with anticipation? Are you 'movable' to be a participant in its coming? We become so familiar with the status quo that we forget that the status quo is temporary.

I make no apology for the fact that again today, the motif is 'waiting'. How we 'wait' in the natural has a profound connection with our prayer lives.

Arrange to meet a friend or colleague somewhere today, but arrive half an hour early. Experience true waiting. Use it as time to pray for the coming of the Kingdom, and give the Holy Spirit space to move you. We all have to wait for many things in life, so why not turn this into a discipline, instead of getting frustrated at a late train or bus. Let the innate tension of waiting lead you always into praying for the 'now, but not yet' of the Kingdom.

NOTES

51

HOMESICK

Make a visit to your local cemetery. Find an appropriate place to sit and read.

I quickly inherited my dad's love for cricket, but living in Northern Ireland afforded us very little chance to see our heroes perform. A couple of years ago I was able to take my Dad to see England play at Lords. It was a fantastic day. As we stood to applaud Andrew Flintoff's vicious century, we looked at each other, and it was just one of those moments that froze in time. I thought to myself, 'I've shared this unbelievable experience with the man who has given me so much, including my passion for this game. To be honest, I can now die happy.'

Read **Luke 2:28-35**

Simeon's faith is such that he is now happy to die. His words are sung in churches all over the world as the Nunc Dimittis, including the amazing statement, 'Lord, now lettest thou thy servant depart in peace, according to thy word' (Lk. 2:29 [KJV]). He has met the Christ and held him in his arms, as God promised he would. He continues 'For my eyes have seen your salvation, which you have prepared in the sight of all people.' His vivid language describing this salvation anticipates a prepared feast that will last forever. You can see why he has no qualms about taking his seat.

I have a simple question. Are you ready to go? Is the promise of God enough, or do you want 'Jesus plus...'? What of this life could possibly better being with him in perfection, now? Or do the pleasures of this world still seem a stronger tug? Or do you believe that God can't do without you down here? We obviously shouldn't be actively trying to shuffle off this mortal coil, but it's a question of attitude. Where is our treasure? Do we genuinely believe it when we say 'to die is gain'? I am a temporary resident of this world. I want my homesickness to be a stronger drive than my love of this place, as then there's just a chance I may begin to see my sufferings and successes in perspective.

Stay seated to pray, or wander through the cemetery. Let your significance and insignificance inform your prayers. Ask God to give you a longing for home. Simeon knew there was one thing in his life that he had to do before he died. Is there one thing you know you need to do before changing states? Sometimes this question helps to bring focus to our multi-tasking lives. If there isn't, perhaps ask God to reveal more of his calling for your life, as you hold it ever more lightly.

NOTES●◆

READY TARGET

Luke 2:34-35

Then Simeon blessed them and said to Mary, his mother: "This child is destined to cause the falling and rising of many in Israel, and to be a sign that will be spoken against, so that the thoughts of many hearts will be revealed. And a sword will pierce your own soul too."

In its original context, the word 'sign' is actually speaking of an archery target that people fire their arrows at. Simeon is prophesying over Jesus, to his mother of all people, that this child will be targeted and attacked. Pretty strong stuff. But this honest, practical prophecy is vital to Mary and Joseph's ability to spiritually and psychologically prepare for what is to come.

Similarly we should be in no doubt as to what will come our way as Christians, if we put our heads above the parapet. Paul warns all the way through his letters that it isn't a matter of 'if' we are persecuted, but a matter of 'when'.

There has been an explosion in the use of sports psychologists in the last few years. Individuals and teams that play at the highest level spend hours doing psychological as well as physical training. Many of the exercises revolve around visualising the scenarios that they will encounter when on the pitch, and rehearsing the mental subroutines required to cope with the pressure. Time after time sportsmen profess that these exercises have been vital to their ability to perform in often very public settings. Will we be prepared when the accusations fly, or the subtle barbs begin? Will we buckle and miss the open goal, or hear the voice telling us 'If God be for us, who can be against us?' and stick the ball in the back of the net? Will we react angrily to a tackle, when we have been intentionally targeted, or remember that our fight is not against flesh and blood?

Draw an archery target and stick it up on your wall to remind you of Jesus' understanding of yours and others situations when you are attacked, however subtly, for your faith. Or buy a dart board.

Visit www.releaseinternational.org.uk and order their newsletters, to enable you to pray for those Christians who are being targeted and persecuted as we speak. Pin the letter up on your target. A friend of mine was recently detained and questioned in a 'moderate' country for three days without food. He didn't give in to the threats made against him and his family if he did not co-operate with a plan to infiltrate and scatter a group of believers there. It is real.

NOTES

53

FIND JESUS

Luke 2:41-51

In our shrink-wrapped culture, we find it almost impossible to believe that Mary and Joseph simply lost track of Jesus for a whole day. But children were often looked after by extended family members and friends in one big interacting throng. The men and women would travel separately, so perhaps they both assumed he was with the other group.

The language used in verse 44 caught my eye especially – 'Thinking he was in their company...' How often do we work on the presumption that we are walking side-by-side with Jesus, when actually he is somewhere else altogether? We get so used to our way of doing things (often successfully) that we get to the point where we don't feel we need to follow Jesus too closely any more. This isn't usually a conscious decision. It just happens gradually and imperceptibly. When was the last time you asked him to direct you in your life? When was the last time you asked him what his priorities were, and in which direction he was moving?

The modern Christmas is an example of how easy it is to lose track of Jesus. In a review of Cliff Richard's song Saviour's Day a few years ago, a music magazine said 'No snow, no Santa, no reindeer? What's this got to do with Christmas?' A friend of mine recently told the story of his wife shouting into the loft to ask what he and his daughter were doing. They had been getting their Christmas decorations out, but there was one figurine missing from the Nativity scene. 'We're looking for Jesus', came the nine-year old reply. It's actually a pretty profound metaphor for most people's Christmas experience.

Go looking for Jesus today. Just wander into your town. His parents looked for him for three days. My suspicion is that you may find him anywhere in your town – in the act of kindness to the lady who has dropped her shopping, in the dedication of those working with people with learning disabilities, in the patience of the traffic warden suffering verbal abuse. To mirror the story, after half an hour's seeking, end your search in a local church. In verse 49, Jesus says, 'Why were you searching for me? Didn't you know I had to be in my Father's house?' Even if this is the church you are a member of, spend some time wandering around and seeking Jesus, looking at the stained glass windows, the plaques and the crosses.

Now spend some time on your knees, seeking Jesus' forgiveness for letting him out of your sight.

NOTES

54

PREPARE THE WAY

Find some woodland in the vicinity of where you live. Try taking a direct route across it, rather than following the paths. Stop somewhere in the midst of it to read **Luke 3:1-18**.

'Preparing the way' does not have the same significance now as it did then. In those days there were often no roads for a King and his entourage to travel down, so some serious clearing or flattening had to occur. It was not merely asking the crowds, 'Would you mind awfully taking a few steps back from the road?' Folks would have understood exactly what John meant when he said 'make straight paths for him'. The nearest we get to this is probably the police officers of London who spread their arms wide, pushing into a crowd to prevent onlookers getting in the way of a victorious team in their open-topped bus.

John's preaching and actions started to clear away some of the rubble that had been developing in the lives of the Jews. Look at his language. This man is not just a policeman, he is a steamroller. He had a passionate message of repentance, calling people away from the selfishness that would blind them to the coming Messiah.

Could you do something today to make the journey smoother for someone? Could you aid them with a simple DIY task, pick something up for them, or just listen to them? Are there people who have little, while you have the equivalent of ten tunics, not just the two that John suggests sharing?

Are there some boulders in your life or others' that are hindering the entrance of the One who will baptise 'with the Holy Spirit and with fire'?

Inspired by the boldness of John the Baptist, name some of these boulders. Spend some time repenting, but don't leave it there. 'Produce fruit in keeping with repentance' (v8).

It may be time to confront people with their need to repent. If you don't do it, who will? But it also worth bearing in mind Jesus' caution on this subject. It was something to do with planks and specks. Make sure that you've got rid of your own heavy masonry before you go looking for toothpicks, and make sure you're doing it for the right reasons. Hopefully it's for the good of the person(s) involved, rather than the desire to get something off your chest. I once wrote a song which questioned my motives on this issue, which probed my heart to see if I really wanted folks to become more like Jesus, or simply more like me, to make my life a little bit easier.

NOTES

55

GOOD WORK

Read this passage in your place of work. Get in early if you have to.

Luke 3:21-22

> When all the people were being baptised, Jesus was baptised too. And as he was praying, heaven was opened and the Holy Spirit descended on him in bodily form like a dove. And a voice came from heaven: "You are my Son, whom I love; with you I am well pleased."

God spoke these words before Jesus began his ministry. So his expression of pleasure is not based on healings, preaching and teaching, but on Jesus' character of simple service, working with his father. The Greek word teknon, that is normally translated 'carpenter' can also be translated as something more akin to an 'odd-job man'. Can you imagine Jesus coming round to fix your light fittings, sort out your boiler, or clear out your shed? Take this on board today as encouragement for the sometimes mundane service of your work. To you it may not feel significant but note Colossians. 3:23: 'Whatever you do, work at it with all your heart, as working for the Lord, not for men.'

It is all too easy to disconnect our 'spiritual' lives from our work. But work is not just what we have to do to survive. It is a God-ordained act of worship, a huge percentage of what we are on the earth to do. God was and is the Ultimate Worker. His work in creation set a pattern for our lives.

See if you can hear his voice over the hum of the photocopier today – 'With you I am well pleased.'

Take time today to encourage one or all of your workmates, and let them know that they are doing a great job. With a little bit of preparation, what about leaving a little postcard (perhaps with a chocolate) on everyone's desk (or somewhere appropriate), pointing out something that you appreciate about them. You will change their day. You will struggle to find something positive to say about some people. Fighting hard to find these things is an important discipline. There is always something you can find. We just need to make the effort to find it. Writing people off is the world's way, not ours.

NOTES

56

VERTIGO

Get yourself to a high place of some description. This could be the top of a hill or a building. A cliff would be perfect.

Read **Luke 4:1-13.**

For anyone who is gifted in certain ways (and that's all of us), it is very easy to rely on those gifts and talents, and not on God. There is a sense of that in what Jesus is being tempted to do in this passage. All that he was asked to do, he could have done. This story provides the subtext for U2's great song Vertigo from How to Dismantle an Atomic Bomb. The vertigo Bono is experiencing comes from being up in that high place and hearing the words 'All of this can be yours...'

The bottom line is that Satan isn't stupid. He doesn't try to tempt us with what he knows we won't do (usually because of social constraints). He may not tempt us to hit someone, but will perhaps tempt us to gossip about them. He may not tempt us to order a dodgy satellite channel, but he may tempt us to leave our eyes hovering over an unhelpful music video. He works by subtle increments.

We have over-simplified and dramatised the events in the desert. Satan doesn't appear in a puff of smoke wearing red leather and holding a pitchfork. He instead sidles up to Jesus as a pious counselling friend, quoting Scripture. It is only at the end of temptation three that he is unmasked, offering a direct bribe, which he doesn't even attempt to wrap up with a scriptural contortion. All our temptation scenarios will probably start with a person or a situation that seems totally rational and respectable, rather than a bloke with horns, or large red Xs appearing in the corner of our vision to warn of impending danger.

Put yourself in Satan's shoes and draw up a master plan on his behalf for how best to tempt you towards or away from certain things. Being an expert on the subject, you probably won't get it far wrong. This will bring some honesty and reality to your 'tempted' life. The best generals or sports coaches study their opponents' strategy at length. Share this plan with an accountable friend, who can help you watch out for the high tackles. This is something we need to talk about a lot, rather than pretend that we are immune from temptation, which is total nonsense, bearing in mind that even Jesus was tempted.

Extra time

Jesus presented a dead straight bat to Satan's temptations by quoting Scripture. Would you be able to quote any verses of Scripture in the direction of the bowler? As a cricketer, it takes hard work and practice to develop the unnatural habit of playing straight, and it takes genuine effort to memorise some Scripture. (As with cricket, it's much easier to just have a swing.) Write out three verses on bits of paper that you will try to memorise during the course of today.

NOTES

57

MY MANIFESTO

Luke 4:14-21

Jesus' quoting of the prophet Isaiah here is often called his manifesto. In an age where political parties promise much but deliver little, it still stands true.

This is my favourite piece of Scripture. As an 18 year old, it simply popped up too many times in various contexts in the space of a three month period for it to be a coincidence. I decided it was to be my manifesto too. Jesus did do all that he promised while in his physical body on the earth, but he still does all that he promised through his 'now body', the church.

We are called, of course, to fulfil this mandate, but do you have a specific manifesto or mission statement for your life? It could start: 'The Spirit of the Lord is upon me, because he has anointed me to...'

This is a powerful exercise in itself, if you let the truth of the phrase 'The Spirit of the Lord is upon me' sink in. In exactly the same way that God's Spirit rested upon Jesus, the Spirit is upon you and me. We don't have to chant some incantation to call for his presence or hope for some future blessing. He is upon us now.

You may want to ask yourself what 'good news' you will bring to people. In an age where the only news that seems to be newsworthy is tragic or scandalous, what hope can you bring? Our individual conversations have become reflections of the news media's tone; often cynical, often complaining, and often miserable, believing that things can't get any better. Can you think of ways that you can change the tone of your conversations? There are amazing things happening all over the world, with lives being turned around, but they often won't be reported. Let's make sure that we do.

Write your manifesto now. Because of our fear of failure, there is tendency in these exercises to just mention vague aspirations. Set specific objectives and targets.

Examples:
- To mentor three young people this year
- To bring two people from work to our housegroup
- To write six chapters of the book I've never started
- To visit an Asian country.

'The Spirit of the Lord is upon me, because he has anointed me to...'

NOTES

58

COMMANDING AUTHORITY

Luke 4:31-37

If I could summarise this passage in one word, (and in fact, I will) it would be 'authority'. The original text in verse 32 can be translated 'speaking as a new lawgiver.' Jesus was not making pleasant suggestions, but commanding.

We often say that some people have 'natural authority'. I do believe that we should pray that God would give us more 'natural' authority in our life situations, but as we make choices for him (that are later proved to be right choices) this authority actually grows naturally. Sometimes this authority only comes when we take a risk and step up into new territory. Jesus took this risk. He was seen as a new lawgiver. We sometimes look at what he said and what he did, forgetting that those around him didn't know what we with the benefit of hindsight now know about him. Those in his vicinity were shocked by this new kid on the block, so the mental and emotional strength Jesus must have needed to keep saying and doing as he knew he should, would have been immense. As we know from these days of 'hero to zero' tabloid reporting, the fact that you are creating a stir makes you all the more likely to be a target for criticism, which he got by the bucket load.

You know that thing that you have been dying to say in a meeting, (be that a board meeting, church meeting, or informal gathering) because you feel it is a key issue, but thus far you've felt too young or not 'highly ranked' enough to say it? Today, say it. We have been given authority in his name. He believes in us. There is a good chance that some of the disciples were still in their twenties.

Luke 9:1-2

> When Jesus had called the Twelve together, he gave them power and authority to drive out all demons and to cure diseases, and he sent them out to preach the Kingdom of God and to heal the sick.

We don't have to wait for anyone else to tell us to go 'do the stuff'. My mate Shaun is a policeman and he often tells me of the mental barrier he has to cross when he is doing something that another human being doesn't want him to do (like arrest him). At these times he has to remember that he is wearing a uniform, that he has a warrant card, and that he is exercising the authority invested in him by law, and not working from any authority of his own. Perhaps we need to bear that in mind more when we have crises of confidence in our faith sharing or Kingdom actions.

NOTES ●✛

59

MAKE WAVES

You need to find a pond or lake.

Luke 4:36-37

> All the people were amazed and said to each other, "What is this teaching? With authority and power he gives orders to evil spirits and they come out." And the news about him spread throughout the surrounding area.

The word used here for 'news' can actually be translated 'sound', and the image is that of a sound spreading into the distance, like a sonar blip, or a handclap in a cathedral. Again, if you remember your physics lessons from school, in a sound wave air is displaced vertically and the sound travels horizontally. (But in a huge variety of directions.)

So find some water and find a pebble or six, and lob them in one at a time. See how long-lasting the effect of a small vertical displacement is on the full breadth of the horizontal pond. The wave is carried to every corner of the pond. This seemed to be the case with the 'sound' of Jesus. As Eugene Petersen puts it, 'Jesus was the talk of the town.'

As you toss each stone, pray for the impact of your words and life on a specific area. Throw a stone for your workplace, a stone for your family, and so on. News travels fast, as they say, especially when it's good news. The ripple effect of the Holy Spirit will carry God's word through you further than you could ever imagine.

NOTES

60

TAKE THE LOW ROAD

Luke 4:38-44

Jesus never takes the soft option. He has never been more popular, after a day of phenomenal miracles. My instinct would be to think, 'things are going well here, let's milk it for a while.' But Jesus sees the big picture and 'he can do only what he sees his Father doing' (Jn. 5:19). Jesus refers to the 'one who sent me' ten times in the Gospels. Talk about a man on a mission, unswayable by the popular opinion expressed in verse 42 – 'they tried to keep him from leaving them.'

The famous proverb springs to mind:

Proverbs 3:5-6
>   Trust in the Lord with all your heart
>   and lean not on your own understanding;
>   in all your ways acknowledge him,
>   and he will make your paths straight.

Sometimes there will be nothing wrong with our understanding. The options we would choose would be good and sensible, but they may not be the best. Our brains and reasoning are useful, but if we always 'lean' on them, eventually the stick breaks. For Jesus in this case, the 'straight path' is away from Capernaum. Are there decisions and situations where you simply continue in 'default mode' because you haven't taken the time to consult God?

When you look at the geography of Jesus' travelling, you realise that he truly was following a divine compass, as it seems to make no obvious strategic sense. If I were him, I'd have headed straight to the major population centre in Galilee, called Tiberias, but there is no record of him visiting there. As far as we know, he also never went to Sepphoris, the capital of Galilee. We always seem to be attracted by key places, big numbers, influential people, and 'success'. I guess 'His ways are not our ways', but be encouraged by Isaiah 2:3. If we let him, 'He will teach us his ways, so that we may walk in his paths.' I often feel that instead of trying to find 'his way', I am merely begging Jesus to come and sing harmony with me on My way.

The secret of Jesus' inch-perfect navigation is revealed in verse 42 – 'At daybreak Jesus went out to a solitary place.' It was this intimate communion with his Father that enabled it. So let's finish by doing something that is definitely following Jesus' way. Finding solitary space is becoming harder and harder in today's world, so don't expect it to come to you. You need actively to go looking for it. Jesus had to go out to find a solitary space. Find somewhere outside where you can be totally alone for at least half an hour. Jesus will have got there before you.

NOTES ●◆

SEASON 2

PART 2

61

THE FUGITIVE

Read **Jonah chapter 1.**

In Hebrew, Jonah means 'dove'. I can't help thinking that there is symbolism here associated with his namesake, who had some ocean-based trouble a few years earlier. Her flight was from Noah and the ark and was also in the vain hope of finding somewhere to rest.

Does this story ring any bells? Running from God is actually often the action of someone who knows God rather well. Like Jonah, you may know his capabilities, and you know your own potential, and to be honest, that's where it gets scary. A close neighbour to the fear of failure that stalks many of our lives is the fear of not fulfilling our potential. This drives us to instead throw our energies into activities or relationships that are well within our limits and need minimum help from God, which is handy, because time with him would remind us of our true calling. Perhaps like Jonah, the stumbling block is that those people or that place we are called to actually stir up emotional angst or prejudice.

Do something today to connect with your Nineveh. It's the place or person with whom you just know you should spend some time, but you always manage to find some other noble thing to do to avoid it. You may need to visit a website, do a Google search, make a phone call, or fill out an application form. The problem is we get quite used to the relative safety of the inside of the whale.

Jonah prays an amazing prayer in chapter 2, the language of which can actually be traced back to ten separate psalms. Even in the darkest place (and this was dark), if our lives have a framework of God's word, it calls our souls to a place that is beyond simply dwelling on the natural world.

Go to the place where you 'hide'. This may be curling up in your bed, or sitting in front of your computer, or in the local pub. There pray Jonah's prayer from chapter 2, and see if God won't hurl you back in the direction you're meant to be going.

Because the dove does eventually find its olive leaf.

NOTES

YOUR STORY

Read the rest of the book of Jonah.

Have you ever wondered who wrote the book of Jonah? Was his secretary stuck in the whale with him? Unless he had a camera crew following him around, there really are only two ways that we could know everything that we do about him in such detail. Either he wrote it himself in the third person (and with his mood swings, I wouldn't be surprised), or he took the time to describe accurately to a scribe what had happened to him.

Have you ever written down your story? The story of how God has taken you from where you were to where you are? We seem to constantly live 'in the moment' these days, and what is most important to us is only what is current. However, we have so much to learn from looking back and appreciating our own journey. What changes have you seen, what blessings have you received? What has been joyful and what has been painful? When did growth happen? Who were the key players? What were the shipwrecks, and what were the moments of bravery? Just because there are no massive mammalian encounters, your story is no less important.

Spend a decent bit of time doing this. As a target, aim for five hundred words, but if it ends up much longer, then no problem. Look to see if there are common themes running through experiences and relationships that perhaps you've never seen before. Once you've done it, share it with someone. You may be surprised how much it will encourage you and others. It may also make you more confident in sharing your story on an ad hoc basis in conversation. However, more than anything else today, simply share your story with God. Rejoice in how he has been faithful. Bring him the highs and the lows, and thank him that at the end of the day, he is the ultimate Author.

NOTES

63

OBSERVING DESERVING

James 1:16-18

Every **good and perfect gift comes from him**. Not just the traditionally 'Christian' things. Every good appliance, piece of art, relationship, or opportunity. Every good design, haircut, recipe or view.

Take a walk and choose to give thanks to God for absolutely everything that you see or for the things that are represented by what you see.

You could use this prayer for each item: 'Lord God, every good and perfect gift comes from you. Thank you.'

NOTES

PLAY YOUR PART

One of the most helpful ways to read the Bible is by stepping into the stories.
Decide before you read a certain passage which character you will be
'playing'. Try to imagine the scene. Complete the picture with mental sound
effects and crowds. Throughout the story, ask yourself these sort of
questions:

What has their life been like up to this point?

How are they feeling?

What are they are thinking?

What is their attitude towards God?

Why and how do all these things change during the course of the story?

What happens next for them?

This style of reading can lead to powerful times of worship as you ask
yourself what words a character would use to describe God at a particular
point in the story. Let these words inform your picture of God's character, and
flow out into worship.

As an example: Read **John 8:1-11,** and 'play' the woman caught in adultery.
Hear the words spoken directly to her.

NOTES

65

IT'S OH SO QUIET

Psalm 37:7

> Be still before the Lord and wait patiently for him;
> do not fret when men succeed in their ways,
> when they carry out their wicked schemes.

Find a room where you can sit in absolute silence for half an hour. Stick it out even if you think of a very, very good reason to get up and do something. ('I'll forget about it if I don't do it now' is probably Satan's most helpful lie to prevent us spending quality time with God.) A helpful tip is keeping pen and paper handy in case you do think of something that you need to do later. Writing it down prevents you worrying about it while you're praying.

There is a pain barrier for most people at about seven or eight minutes, at which point many of us run away, but if you get through that wall then the subsequent time becomes much easier. It takes that long to let the thoughts of our mind settle down and for our spirits to engage. Just 'be' with God. Much of the change in the disciples' lives came not just from Jesus' teaching but the impact of simply being in his presence. Another benefit of silence is that most of us are much better listeners when we're not talking.

Changing posture during a time of silence may be helpful. Certain positions enable us to be in a more 'receptive' mode – e.g. Open-handed or lying on our backs, while others speak more of reverence – e.g. lying prostrate or kneeling. Sitting can reinforce 'resting' in God, and walking can accentuate the sense of his present reality, rather than the potentially 'virtual reality' of having our eyes closed. Try spending ten minutes in each of a range of positions.

Actively seeking silence is a vital spiritual discipline in twenty-first century living. As Ronald Rolheiser explains in his book, The Shattered Lantern,[8] our egos are scared of silence in the same way that they fear death, because they can 'do' no more then. Where will our value come from, if we cannot 'do'? But the soul rejoices in the freedom of death and the freedom of silence. It is no longer chained to the tasks which must be fulfilled to salve our self-esteem.

Come to God today not looking for any answers or favours. Just come. Leave your agenda at the door. Wait patiently.

NOTES

66

LIFT THE LABEL

Proverbs 31:8

> Speak up for those who cannot speak for themselves, for the rights of all who are destitute.

Check the labels of the clothes you are wearing (perhaps as you're putting them on). Where are they from? The likelihood is that they have been manufactured somewhere in South-East Asia. Feed your discoveries through to the website. In Bangladesh I saw 'Made in Germany' and 'Made in the USA' labels being sewn onto clothes. I also saw the conditions that many garment workers have to work in, and you definitely handle your clothes differently when you realise how many hands have actually touched them before you. Many workers in Bangladesh receive less than £5 a week. They would need twice that amount to be able to afford basic essentials, like food, healthcare and accommodation. This is the case for millions of clothing industry workers around the world.

Profits are being put before people – and many workers (90% of whom are women) are trapped in the cycle of poverty as a result. Add to this the horrendous conditions in many of the factories, and well, how are your clothes feeling on you right now?

A great way to get involved is by joining Tearfund's 'Lift the Label' campaign. They are calling on UK clothes retailers to join the Ethical Trading Initiative, asking companies to take responsibility for ensuring that the people making the clothes they sell work in safe and healthy conditions, are paid a wage they can live on, have the right to organise themselves into trade unions, and speak out to improve conditions. Add your voice today via www.tearfund.org/youth, then following the links.

This is a fantastic way to quite literally 'Speak up for those who cannot speak for themselves'. In terms of the global market economy, their voices are the quietest whisper compared to our booming voices, so let's make ourselves heard.

Pray for God to lead you to other voiceless people in our society and in the wider world who you could 'speak up' for.

For more information regarding fairly traded clothes, check out the website for a full list of retailers. Peopletree (www.ptree.co.uk) and www.nosweatapparel.com have built up great reputations.

NOTES●✦

67

ELEPHANTINE FORGIVENESS

Read **Matthew 18:21-35.**

The phrase 'forgive and forget' is not in the Bible. There is plenty of forgiving going on, but forgetting is not once listed in its vicinity. In fact, I think that phrase undermines the cost and central thrust of forgiveness. Amos 8:7 says, 'The Lord has sworn by the Pride of Jacob: "I will never forget anything they have done."' Forgiveness is not a casual thing. It cost Jesus his life to provide it for us. Hebrews 9:22 says, 'In fact, the law requires that nearly everything be cleansed with blood, and without the shedding of blood there is no forgiveness.'

Forgiveness is not about saying, 'Oh, that's all right, it wasn't that hurtful, you're fine.' It's about saying, 'Yes, that wasn't good. It hurt me. But I have freely received forgiveness, so I am going to "give it on" to you.' That literally is forgiving. Giving on what you have received.

There is an episode of The Simpsons where Marge is in prison, and for handiness, instead of tidying up properly, Bart and Lisa quite literally sweep everything under the carpet. At the outset it works, but eventually they are surfing across their living room on a tide of trash. We often employ this handy option to keep the peace, but if you ignore what it is that has hurt, it prevents the power of the cross coming to bear on it. Little things that people say or do gradually accumulate until relationships suffer crisis moments. We've never addressed the issues, often with our closest friends and family, because we've confused forgiving with ignoring. I recently experienced this in a situation where someone had been annoying me more and more over a period of months. I thought I was so impressively restrained in staying quiet on the subject, but then one day, a straw broke this camel's back and I exploded into an unpleasant contorted version of myself.

Are there some folks who you need to 'forgive from the heart', not just the head? This will involve privately letting go to God, but sometimes will mean contacting them. In any conversations that ensue, you may well discover that you need to ask their forgiveness too.

Pray for the grace and the boldness to confront and forgive. Too often we just do one or the other.

NOTES

POPULAR

Many of today's big political speeches are tested on focus groups to ascertain which sections are making the listeners 'feel good'. Phrases are edited or removed if they don't meet with high percentage approval. About two thousand years ago on a hillside a man delivered a speech that would have failed almost every test that a pollster could throw at it. Towards the end of it, he challenges a lot of assumptions and 'raises the bar' beyond where any of his listeners would have been comfortable. I can imagine the slashes of red pen his spin doctors would have put throughout the text. 'You can't say that.'

Read **Matthew 5**. Read it as a speech, as that is what it was. You could shoot a video of yourself delivering it, then watch it back.

Let's face it. Most of us are people-pleasers. We care more about what people think of us than perhaps anything else. Our credibility and image are like strait-jackets preventing us from challenging the status quo. How do we change from being people-pleasers to God-pleasers?

Analyse the decisions you make today, and assess what part pleasing people had in those decisions. When did we make that journey that all children seem to make from wanting to please our fathers and mothers, to caring more about pleasing our peers? Is it fear of people, is it fear of conflict, is it a desire to be popular? Reflect on how little these factors impacted Jesus' life. He never sought human approval, checking for applause after a miracle, or scavenging through his email feedback for affirmation. However, the journey should not end with the phrase 'God-pleaser'. We can seek God's approval just as unhealthily as we seek other people's. Jesus was never seeking his Father's approval through his ministry. He knew that he had it. Let the truth that you don't have to work for his approval rise above any other temptation to go looking for it from others.

Another example of people-pleasing taking second place in the Bible is when Peter and John were called before the Sanhedrin, and received some seemingly absolute news in Acts 4:19, 'Then they called them in again and commanded them not to speak or teach at all in the name of Jesus.'

Peter and John take absolutely no heed of this edict, even though there were many practical reasons why it would have been a good idea. When they are hauled back in, Acts 5:29 sums up their reply. "We must obey God rather than men.'

Make a list of 'false absolutes' like this, that you have begun to believe, that prevent you speaking or acting as you are called. Examples could be –
'It's unprofessional to mention your faith at work.'
'People don't want leadership any more.'

Bring before God the decisions you made today, and your honest assessment of them, regarding people-pleasing. Ask that he would give you the strength to make that journey from people-pleasing to God-fearing.

NOTES

PART 2

SEASON 2

69

STRESS BYPASS

Philippians 4:6-7 (KJV)

> Be careful for nothing; but in everything by prayer and supplication with thanksgiving let your requests be made known unto God. And the peace of God, which passeth all understanding, shall keep your hearts and minds through Christ Jesus.

Do you remember Swampy, the environmental activist? He achieved nationwide notoriety by refusing to move from the little caves that he had created in land that was about to become the Newbury bypass. At the time it got me thinking about that word 'bypass'. It struck me that it quite accurately sums up what is being articulated in these verses from Philippians. God's peace quite literally has the ability to bypass our understanding. It takes a route well around the crazy city centre traffic of our brains to get straight to its destination – our soul and spirit. It literally brings peace and calm when our reasoning has no reason for peace and calm. That is God's peace.

It doesn't attempt to fight through the crowded streets of our brains, trying to sort out the issues. It knows that there will always be issues. So often we let the chaos of our random thought patterns determine much more than they should, and in effect become prisoners to the gridlock of our minds.

Take some sheets of A4 paper. On each piece of paper name a 'stress city' that represents an area of your life where stress takes over. Perhaps with the help of a close friend, decide on and draw in some useful 'bypasses' that will allow you to avoid the mental traffic. Sometimes these will be actions, and sometimes this will mean inaction. At these times, give your friend the permission to suggest the 'bypass' rather than the 'route through town'. For instance, when a certain person is stressing a friend of mine, the bypass route I suggest is finding a reason to leave the room for a few moments to deflate the tension, then coming back in with the intention of bringing Jesus back into the room. Sometimes a few moments' space is all that is required to get a bit of perspective.

Pray that the peace of God would when necessary, bypass your understanding.

NOTES ●◆

70

ABOUT TIME

Deuteronomy 32:7

> Remember the days of old;
> consider the generations long past.
> Ask your father and he will tell you,
> your elders, and they will explain to you.

I saw a beautiful West End show recently called Young at Heart. It consisted of a group of senior citizens aged 75-93 singing their hearts out (not literally) in the rendering of classic rock songs. What was most poignant was that for me many of the words of heartbreak and love found much deeper resonance than when I had heard them uttered by scrawny twenty-somethings first time round. When the older folks sang these familiar words, they had a strangely profound impact. Something told me that these people knew the reality of real commitment and real suffering.

We are a proud generation who believe that because we have more knowledge than previous generations, we are not in need of their wisdom. Very wrong. A wise man once said 'Experience is what you get when you don't get what you want.' There is an innate wisdom that only comes from experience. When was the last time you consulted someone older than yourself for some wisdom? It is a phenomenally important discipline. You may think you don't need it, but older, wiser people ask you the questions that you hadn't even realised you needed to answer. That's the whole point. Why make the same mistakes or miss the same opportunities that those who have gone before us did? What a waste that would be.

Prayer

You many want to confess a wrong attitude to the generations above you, or ask for guidance towards those whose wisdom you will benefit from.

Make plans today to simply spend some time with an older, wiser Christian. Get the date in your diary.

NOTES

PART 2

SEASON 2

HIDDEN TREASURE

Acts 17:24-27

Organise a game of hide and seek, or a treasure hunt of some description.

God desires us to seek him, but often the reason we don't seek him is that we have lost our appetite for seeking in general. What was your reaction to the first sentence? Have you lost your desire to play, to hunt, to search? Did that end with childhood or student days? We expect all experiences or information to come to us on a plate these days. Yes, we like the view at the top of the mountain but we can't be bothered with the effort to get there, so we'll take the cable car. God reveals to us in these verses that sometimes the seeking experience is the experience. It teaches us to trust him. The great thing is that in reality, God isn't actually very good at hide and seek. He is always bigger than whatever he hides behind.

On returning from your treasure hunt, use a concordance or enter the word 'seek' into a web-based Bible search program like www.biblegateway.com. Meditate on the verses that you find in light of your 'seeking experience'.

- Did your seeking stop when things got difficult?
- In general, how much do you let circumstances distract your seeking of God?
- How did it feel once you found what you were looking for?
- Do you revel in the excitement of the unknown, or do you fear it?
- Do you fear not being in control of a situation?
- Seeking, by definition, takes effort. Do we make an effort when we seek?
- Does God hide?
- If not, why would he call us to seek him?

Spend some time seeking him in prayer, as you reflect on your answers.

NOTES

EARTHLY TREASURE

Acts 2:45

> Selling their possessions and goods, they gave to anyone as he had need.

Why do we attach so much importance to accumulating stuff? We'd like to think we don't, but most of our houses tell a more honest story, with a kitchen appliance or receptacle for every conceivable emergency culinary situation. Enough garments to clothe a small town in Finland. Enough technology to entertain, inform and distract us from the real world until the year 2035. Jesus is very clear about where our investment should be and has the audacity to link our ability to invest in the Kingdom with our over-the-top desire to invest in our comfort or perceived security here on earth.

So have a 'life laundry'. Sell off (perhaps via eBay) all the things that, with honest reflection, are simply 'treasures on earth', then invest that cash in some heavenly treasure, be that paying for a friend to have a holiday, sponsoring a child, supporting an aid agency, or enabling your church to make more of an impact in your community.

Doing this is important, but it's also deeper than that. It's not merely about the money. Read Matthew 6:19-21.

Our accumulation of stuff or selfish experiences reveals a heart position that is earth-centred. A major reason for this is the way that society has evolved. The sort of heart change and life change that God desires for us is not meant to be possible in the context of individualised lives. Read Acts 2:42-45. Heaven-oriented living requires community and sharing.

Could you resolve with another family to share some household appliances or even DVDs/CDs? Shock – no – we want to be able to use that or watch that whenever we decide to. To paraphrase something that was never true anyway, it would seem that 'handiness is next to godliness'. We want to be in control. God calls us to another way – the way that doesn't have a TV in every bedroom – the way that shares a lawnmower – the way that pays for someone else's MOT when they can't afford it.

After your decisions, read Luke 12:27-30.

NOTES

LOST

Luke 15:11-32

Everyone can identify with being lost. It is an awful feeling. Without a stable frame of reference, everything else in our lives feels fragile. It's partly why the TV series Lost has been so successful. People connect with that underlying tension. Close your eyes and remember the last time you were frustratedly making left turns, then right turns, but not getting any closer to your destination.

All of us know people who have somehow 'got lost'. I know how hard it can be to re-connect. The usual clichés and pat answers don't cut it for someone who has already been 'inside the fold' of Christianity.

Bite the bullet today and get back in touch with someone whom you have lost contact with. Just say hello. Just open a line of communication. Don't force it. Ask God to get busy drawing that son or daughter back home. If you can be a companion for some of that journey then great, but praying may well be the most important thing you can do.

As a further prayer exercise, go into a large estate in your town. Don't take a map or compass. Get deep into this uncharted territory. Experience the frustration of not being able to find your way out. Let your 'lostness' inform your prayers for your friends who are still 'lost'. Simply spend some time bringing them before God, as you wander through trying to find your way back. Pray that they may also find that way home. Pray that their Father would be able to say of them, 'They were lost, but now are found.'

NOTES

CALLING IN A BLESSING

Romans 12:14

> Bless those who persecute you; bless and do not curse.

Is there space for God in your life as a consumer? Logistical frustrations are a regular part of life in a service-based economy – e.g. returning broken items to shops or sorting out faulty mobile phones. As the recorded message tells you for the twenty-fourth time that 'your call is important to us', you feel your blood approaching boiling point. When the time comes for human communication, do you leave God out of the equation? Sure, we should expect systems to work and report it when they don't, but in our headlong rush for 'justice', do we sometimes forget that there is another human being on the other end of the phone who is merely doing their job?

In this situation, many people either recoil from the conflict, or escalate it with increased volume and rudeness. There is nothing more counter-cultural than politely disagreeing with someone. But it's sadly very rare. In the face-to-face scenario, contradicting with a smile goes a long way.

Today, call someone in a call centre (there are thousands to choose from). Ask them how they are, encourage them, and tell them that you are going to pray that people would treat them with respect and understanding, and that they'd simply have a good day. You might want to start by empathising with them, stating how you realise what a hard job they have to do for little thanks. You may be the difference between someone blessing or cursing everyone they speak to for the rest of the day.

Another thought – a guy I know uses the opportunity of 'cold callers' to offer the caller the 'great offer' or free gift of Jesus in return. You can imagine the conversation. 'Well since you're randomly offering me, a complete stranger, your great offer, let me tell you about.......' He does it sensitively of course. The context seems to create a level playing field of privacy invasion. I'll leave the decision about doing this one up to you.

NOTES

75

DAYDREAM, BELIEVER

Take some time to remember what your predominant childhood dream was.
For me, it was an overriding desire to be an astronaut. You don't have to spend
too long flicking through the stories I wrote in school to realise that part of me
was always 'out there.' (Some would say I still am.) In the cold light of day, I now
realise with some sadness that this dream is not going to become reality, but
today I want to encourage you to re-dream. Part of the reason why many of our
childhood dreams fail to materialise is that they are based on a limited grasp of
what is likely or possible. But this is also their beauty. The child's mind sees only
opportunities and potential. The problem is that as adults we begin to subscribe
to unhelpful levels of cynicism, allowing the world to limit our horizons.

Matthew 19:26
> Jesus looked at them and said, "With man this is impossible, but with
> God all things are possible."

Matthew 17:20
> "I tell you the truth, if you have faith as small as a mustard seed, you
> can say to this mountain, 'Move from here to there' and it will move.
> Nothing will be impossible for you."

Jesus wasn't joking when he talked about moving mountains. The problem
is that he's ready to push them while we're still asking him to flatten our
molehills. 'Look up.' He's saying. 'You have bigger fish to fry.' Can we make
the transition from merely existing to truly living? From maintenance to
mission, from management to leadership, and from budgeted plans to faith-
requiring dreams?

Now that we are more schooled in the ways of the world, what better time
to dream? It has been said that those who dream, practise the art of 'seeing

what is yet unseen.' Ask God for new dreams and spend some minutes actively dreaming. Allow yourself to continue through the day. It's a mark of where we've got to as a society that 'day-dreaming' is considered a negative characteristic. Only by stepping out of the rough and tumble of a system can you imagine ways to tinker with or subvert the system. Many top CEOs now take a 'power hour' doing nothing but sitting in silence in a room. If you include God in that hour, then something that is already potent becomes potentially explosive.

Joel 2:28
> I will pour out my Spirit on all people.
> Your sons and daughters will prophesy,
> your old men will dream dreams,
> your young men will see visions.

Dreams can die very quickly, so at the first opportunity, share your new dreams (or your reinstated dreams) with someone you know well.

NOTES

MAKING THE GOOD NEWS NEWS

Romans 10:14

> How, then, can they call on the one they have not believed in? And how can they believe in the one of whom they have not heard? And how can they hear without someone preaching to them?

Part of my job these days is trying to make the 'good news' news. All over the UK, churches and Christian groups are having a massive impact on their communities, but often the only column inches the church gets revolve around controversy.

You can make a difference. Try to develop relationships with the news and feature editors of your local newspaper and radio stations. If you provide one good story or comment, they will keep coming back to you for further material.

In general, local press are much more open to stories than national press, because they have the space to be so, without thousands of press releases flying under their noses everyday. Often they are desperate for decent stories, as you can probably guess from the classic 'Ice cream van driver found without licence' type headlines. So you will actually be helping them out, if you can provide information about events or programs that are having a positive effect.

The importance of us 'getting the word out' like this was rammed home to me while touring with Youth For Christ's band, TVB, visiting a different school every week. It was usually only on the Wednesday or the Thursday that you felt you were really getting through and communicating some truth about the Christian faith. This was because we had to spend Monday and Tuesday deconstructing some of the myths, stereotypes and misconceptions about Christianity before folks would even open their ears to hear. Where do these beliefs come from? Mostly from the media. So it is strategically vital that we inject positive stories about Christianity and Christians into media outlets, not just for PR purposes but because the good news is legitimate news. If there were more positive role models and reference points, then we'd have many fewer hurdles in our normal interaction with folks who aren't yet Christians.

Sometimes we have become so immunised to the power of the gospel transforming lives that we start to take it for granted. When I tell media folks about the sort of projects that British Youth For Christ are involved in, and the sort of change that we see in young people, they are often amazed, and say things like 'We had no idea this sort of thing was going on.'

As a quick check for what will convince an editor that a story is worthwhile, use this acronym – TRUTH. Before sending it, ask yourself if the story is
– Topical
– Relevant
– Unusual
– Trouble (naming a problem then a solution)
– Human

So get out there and tell the story. (And make sure you get a good photograph to go with it – they are vital.)

NOTES

77

WHO CHOSE WHOM?

Grab your TV remote control. Flick around your channels or teletext pages for a few minutes. Exercise your 'right' to choose. Now read John 15:9-17.

With regard to choice we seem to live in a paradox. We make so many choices everyday that we begin to believe that our choice to follow God is just another one of those choices. It is the inevitable product of a consumer society which champions choice as a virtue and an economic driver. Yet we who choose so independently still desperately desire to be chosen, to be selected, to be picked out. We still have memories of being the last one standing when school teams were picked, or of the first time a boy asked us to dance. Feeling chosen is intensely important to us. Into this paradox steps Jesus with 'You did not choose me, but I chose you' (Jn.15:16), but to see the depth of this we need some context.

In Rob Bell's book Velvet Elvis,[9] he describes how only the best of the best of young Jewish scholars would make it through the various levels of Hebrew education to the point where they could ask for an interview with a Rabbi. During this interview, the Rabbi would discern if they had what it took to be one of his select followers. So can you see what a world-inverting experience it would have been for some uneducated fishermen to have a Rabbi walk straight up to them and inform them that he is choosing them.

Do you respond best to blanket instructions aimed at a large group or to a personal phone call commissioning you to a specific task? I suspect we all operate better when we know we are doing a job we have been individually asked to do. There is a conferred sense of status and identity. Can you hear the call? Can you believe he has selected you? Because 'many are invited, but few are chosen' (Mt. 22:14) and 'small is the gate and narrow the road that leads to life, and only a few find it (Mt. 7:14).

And notice the authority that comes with being chosen – "This is my Son, whom I have chosen; listen to him" (Lk. 9:35). This is the Father speaking publicly about Jesus during the multi-media spectacle we sometimes call the Transfiguration. Jesus is God, yet the Father is underlining the amazing truth that Jesus is chosen, so perhaps we need to know it too. At our core.

There is a song called All I Am by a dodgy Irish singer-songwriter called Andy Flannagan. It contains the words 'I am broken, but I am chosen, for you have spoken grace to me.' You could meditate on or sing these words until they sink in beyond your mind to your heart.

NOTES

PART 2

SEASON 2

78

SUPERMARKET SWEEP

I'm always looking out for areas of our lives where we can give God more access, especially if they are areas where we don't normally think about him. This is an example.

Proverbs 23:23

> Buy the truth and do not sell it;
> get wisdom, discipline and understanding.

Get down to your local supermarket. As ever, bring the book and yourself.

How much praying or God-awareness is going on when you're in the supermarket? When those automatic doors slide open, are you purely and simply in 'task mode'? If he prompted you to speak to someone, or help someone, would you be in a place to hear? Or are you tunnel-visioned like I often am? Do you become a bargain hunter with little thought for your health or the health of food producers around the world? Is God there in your trolley or whimpering in the car like a forgotten puppy?

God wants us to share every part of our lives with him, so I know God wants us to enjoy shopping with him. There is a real freedom in talking to God (privately) in a public place, and much thankfulness to be conveyed for what greets our eyes. Can you believe the diversity of foodstuffs that are presented to us these days? Sometimes I simply love looking at them all, without the slightest intention of purchasing. I'm thinking 'God, thank you so much for all this provision. We are so blessed.'

So, pray your way around the aisles for the next twenty minutes or so, giving thanks for the products and praying for the parts of the world represented by them. Pray for those folks who suffer greatly in developing countries, to give us the luxury of cheap food. Give thanks that you have money to spend. Speak to the store management, asking that they stock products with the 'Fairtrade' mark. These days it goes far beyond bananas and chocolate. You can keep up to date with what produce is available via www.fairtrade.org.uk.

If you feel you need to push an empty trolley around with you, to get into the vibe, then go for it. If you actually need stuff, then feel free to grab. Hopefully the next time you're back, your praying self will have more of a chance of kicking in.

You could apply this thought to all types of shopping. Or would God ask us too many awkward questions like, 'Do you need this, or do you simply want it?' When did we start believing that 'retail therapy' was detachable from our spiritual lives? Once you get home, show Jesus around your house as a kind of 'virtual estate agent'. Do every room. How would you explain the need for everything that he finds? Are we counter-cultural, or merely clinging to the culture of the counter?

NOTES

PART 2

SEASON 2

79

REAL REFRESHMENT

This is a simple discipline to still our wandering bodies and keep us in a place of contemplative prayer. Fill a jug with water. Take it with a glass to a place where you won't be disturbed. Nip to the loo before you go (very important). The idea is that you will stay in that spot till you finish the jug. Sometimes it's good to give ourselves targets and discipline to increase our spiritual stamina. Open your Bible to John 4:1-30, to read and drink, savouring the truth and refreshment of the 'spring of water welling up to eternal life.'

It was probably quite easy for you to obtain your glass of water. You turned on the tap and it was there. For Jesus to get his life-giving water to the Samaritan woman, he had to traverse a few dams. He shouldn't have been speaking to her because (1) she was a Samaritan, (2) she was a woman, and (3) she was at a well. Ancient Jewish writings speak of 'old Jews wanting wives' who would frequent the wells where young women came to draw water (a traditional role). Because of this, wells could also be the 'red light districts' of an area. Are you beginning to see how bad this could look for Jesus? This is evidenced by the stunned reaction of the disciples on their return. But Jesus has a divine appointment to bring eternal refreshment, and nothing will stand in his way.

Take some time. Savour the water as you drink, giving thanks that Jesus is willing and able to leap the hurdles that you put in the way of him bringing you eternal refreshment.

Now ask yourself if there are any obstacles that stop you bringing 'the water of life' to people. Often those most in need of water smell the worst. We can always find many rational reasons to not help a beggar, or offer someone a bed for the night, or even lend someone our car. Ask God to remove these obstacles, which are usually always about our own pride and control.

Steve Turner's poem sums this up beautifully –

The God Letters

The Lord God says:
'Share your bread
with the hungry,
bring the homeless poor
into your house,
cover the naked.'

Dear Lord God,
We have got
new carpets,
so this will
not be possible.

©2002 rejesus ltd

Stay in that place until you've finished the jug. Leave space and time for God to speak to you and refresh you with his life-giving water.

NOTES

SEASON 3

PART 1: LUKE

80

MISSION IMPOSSIBLE

Read Luke 5:1-11 in your place of work.

You know when you are in the presence of 'the Holy'. Peter and all his comrades knew that what had just happened was 'supernatural' by anyone's standards. There were no second thoughts when the moment came to follow this amazing man. We are all naturally drawn to those people who amaze and inspire us. When was the last time you dropped everything and followed someone or something?

Often we forget that the imagery used in the Bible was used because it was relevant to the time, place and people involved. If we limit ourselves to thinking that this imagery is exclusive, we limit how God can break into the mindsets of our everyday lives. We forget that images are simply that – images. No image claims to tell the whole truth. There was a moment when God was likened to a shepherd for the first time. There would have been an initial period when people said, 'Shepherd? But God doesn't work for anyone, and shepherds can't do miracles.' Widen your nets to find imagery that expresses who God is to your generation. Sometimes I think God is like the perfect mobile phone network.

Jesus told the disciples that he would make them 'fishers of men.' You can bet your life that the disciples could (1) 'get inside' the image (understanding its nuances), and (2) were regularly reminded of it as they fished. Imagine if Jesus came to you in your place of work today and announced that he was going to involve you in his plan for the Kingdom coming on earth. What would he say? What image would he use that would be relevant to you? If you happen to be a fisherman, then this is easy. What would he say to a journalist? Perhaps 'I will make you a publisher of good news' or to an advertising executive, 'You will draw men to me.' Spend some time working out what he would say and let that influence your daily reality.

As a final thought, reflect on the joy that Simon Peter must have experienced when he saw Jesus' promise become reality. On that Pentecost day, I am sure his mind's eye saw a net extending out over the thousands who were listening to him, drawing them into the Kingdom boat.

Now attempt to put this thinking into practice. Use something that you see in your place of work as the springboard for some imagery that could describe God to someone who doesn't know him. One example when I did this was my amazement at the incessant ticking of the office clock. I prayed – 'God, you are like that clock. You never stop. You are constant and reliable. Your grace is new every second of every minute, and you will keep me going for ever.' This can also be a useful worship exercise for a small group.

NOTES ●◆

REACH OUT

Luke 5:12-15

The man with leprosy in the story has the faith to believe that Jesus can heal him, but I suspect that even he didn't expect Jesus to do it by touching him. He was one of the 'untouchables'. People would intentionally cross the street when they saw him coming. He had been deprived of that most basic human need for contact and connection.

If you can do it appropriately, then don't touch or let yourself be touched by anyone today. Experience the emotional prison it creates. Experience the rejection and the exclusion. Experience the relief and the joy at the moment when someone does finally touch you. Having been avoided by hundreds of sinful people all his life, the leper was touched by the sinless one.

I will never forget being in a leprosy hospital in Bangladesh, being introduced to various patients with ugly, gnarled limbs. We all hovered a safe distance behind the doctor who was introducing the patients. We had gone all the way down one side of the ward when something amazing happened. Ben, one of the guys in our party, simply took two strides forward and shook the hand of the last patient. It was like a dam bursting. Suddenly limbs were being extended to limbs all over the ward. I saw Jesus that day. Are there people in your local community that are never touched by human hand? Are there folks trapped in a downward spiral who you'd rather not be within five yards of, never mind touch? The local priest was the arbiter of who was 'clean' and 'unclean', so by sending the man off to see him, Jesus is making sure that this man is reinstated in his community as well as being healed of leprosy.

HIV/AIDS has been called a 'modern day leprosy', because of the shameful ostracising of its sufferers. My friend Tré helps to run a charity called www.engagehivaids.com. Log on and discover how you can be part of reaching out.

NOTES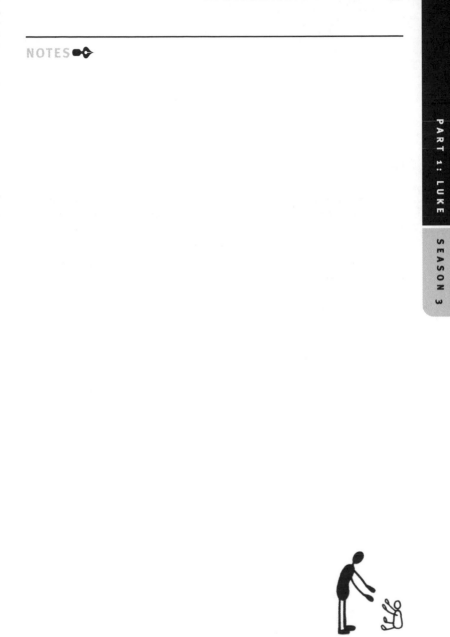

FAITHFUL FRIENDSHIP

Luke 5:17-26

How far would you go for a friend? Both the persistence and the faith of the friends are key here. 'Each to their own' has become an accepted lie in our culture. Is there a situation where you need to be persistent with a friend, and have faith for them on their behalf? Perhaps they have given up on their dreams, or are becoming preoccupied with a relationship (or lack of a relationship). Perhaps you need to actually take them to Jesus, because they have no strength left to get there themselves. You may have to persist, because initially they may not like it.

Make contact with a friend who is in a situation like this today and suggest taking them somewhere; out for coffee, out to the cinema, perhaps to a small group or a church gathering. It may feel awkward, but take encouragement from the bed-lowering friends who didn't take no for an answer, didn't mind creating a scene, and found a way in.

Bring some other friends before Jesus in prayer right now. Carry them right into his presence. Just leave them there. He will do the rest.

NOTES

83

HOSPITALISED

Luke 5:27-32

When I worked as a doctor, one of the most frustrating aspects of the job was folks who were affectionately known as 'timewasters'. Not that these people didn't have problems or need a listening ear, but they stopped you spending as much time as you should have on the people who needed your help in a hurry. I think Jesus is experiencing that same frustration here when the Pharisees in effect ask him the ridiculous question, 'Why do you spend all your time with those who really need help?' I can almost imagine Jesus slapping his forehead and going 'Duhhhh…, don't you get it? Let me get on with my job.'

You see there will always be massive physical, mental, spiritual and emotional needs within a church. We could easily spend our lives admirably addressing these, but become stuck in 'maintenance' mode rather than 'mission' mode. Do we ever think about that provocative statement that the church is the only organisation that exists for the benefit of those who don't belong to it?

Jesus was clear about his calling, but also about the need: "It is not the healthy who need a doctor, but the sick. I have not come to call the righteous, but sinners to repentance." It seems to me that in the church, we are often like hospital managers excited about the efficiency and cleanliness of our hospital, with only one problem. The hospital is full of (mostly) healthy people. I'm not for a moment saying that we should ignore the needs inside the church, but it's a matter of striking the right balance. Perhaps this will help.

Do an audit of the people you know right now. Not the people you would like to know, just the people that you regularly spend time with. On the left of a page list the Christians and on the right list the folks who aren't yet Christians. We lose our edge when we aren't interacting in a meaningful way with those who don't know God yet. The sure-fire way to the truth on this issue is to flick through all the numbers in your mobile phone. No matter what you might claim, these are the people that matter to you and that you regularly connect with. Count how many you have in total, and how many of the numbers belong to Christians. Write down the percentage. Enter it in the survey on the website.

Be accountable to a close friend and together make plans to change this state of affairs, if things are lop-sided. Pray that God would give you natural appointments to treat 'the sick', through common interests such as sports teams, work situations or community groups. Having listed all those names, this is a good chance to pray for the folks on that list, or stick it on your wall, to enable you to pray regularly for people. During spare moments on a train, I often scroll through the address book on my phone to give me some raw material for prayer.

NOTES

NEW WINESKINS

Luke 5:36-39

In this post-modern age, we have a great need for new methods of discovering and celebrating the same old truths. Time and time again I have seen the enthusiasm and energy of new believers poured into old structures that were designed for another time. The result has been disastrous. The new people are spilt, and the old structure is also damaged and hurt.

In what contexts do you meet with other Christians and where? Is it worth changing the venue or size or shape to make it more accessible to someone who has never been near a gathering of Christians? Could you meet in a park, or in the function room of a pub? Could males and females meet separately? Could you 'meet' while sharing a meal? Could people meet up in their place of work? Could you pray via 'Skype' online (www.skype.com)? Could you meet in an afternoon, early morning or weeknight?

The reason there are so many variations in how Christians meet together in various denominations all over the world is partly due to the fact that there is variety in how 'church' is played out in the New Testament. People met in many different contexts and shapes. What a waste therefore, if we get stuck in one particular expression of what church looks like, rather than enjoying the flexibility we are allowed.

For you, this 'shape-shifting' could mean getting a new translation of the Bible, or changing the time or the place where you regularly take time out with God. Give some energy to finding new locations especially, as the change in dynamic this provides keeps your devotional life from becoming stale.

Try out a new wineskin this week.

NOTES

85

CIRCLE OF FRIENDS

If you're like me, you feel as if you never have enough time to see all the people you want to see, or even more worryingly, all the people who want to see you. That's usually where the problems start. People can have you closer to the centre of their circle than they are in yours, or vice versa. Jesus was very honest and structured about his relationship-forming. He had a 'tight' crew of three, a wider group of twelve and then many other disciples. Frustration was limited because most of the time everyone knew where they stood. Jesus didn't promise (explicitly or implicitly) anything beyond what he could deliver, which is where we often get into trouble.

However, narrowing it down to the twelve was hard work. He put in nigh on twenty-four hours of solitary prayer before calling out the twelve. That's about two hours per person, by my reckoning. That's much more effort than the judges on the X-Factor or Pop Idol put in to winnow the thousands down to the few. Rather than having a strong sense of which particular people we are called to share life with, we often use the 'scattergun' technique, whereby we work on the basis of keeping everyone happy, spreading ourselves thinly in the hope of somewhere hitting on some significant relationships.

Now read **Luke 6:12-16.**

Tonight take a long time to pray about not who would be the easiest people to be with, or who needs you the most (the most common deciding factors) but whom God would call you to share your life with; twelve key people whom you will influence and who will influence you. If you have a hillside in the vicinity, go there. The intentionality and the space it will give you will be important. You may already know who these folks are, but it will help your commitment to them to put it on paper.

NOTES

TURN THE WORLD UPSIDE DOWN

Luke 6:20-26

The world is being turned upside-down. The coming Kingdom looks unlike any earthly kingdom. Sounds great, doesn't it? There is such a 'levelling', bringing true justice. The first will be last and the last will be first. I can almost hear the cheering from the crowd.

But hang on, Jesus is still going, and he's talking to me.

Read on through verses 27-31. It would appear that I'm not going to be a spectator as this new world order approaches, but part of its coming. Eeek! That's a different proposition. We all agree the world needs to be changed, but will we agree to change our worlds? And it's not simple stuff either. Does he really expect me to love my enemies?

Today, actively love an 'enemy' or someone you find it hard to get along with. Do good to them. Pray for them. Often when we bring people before God in prayer, we see his heart for them and it becomes more difficult to look negatively upon them. Try it. The hardest part is melting the initial frost, which may have built up over days or weeks of non-communication. Discovering whether or not we have the capacity to love our enemies is actually key to us seeing if what we have in us is truly 'love' or just a reactive warmth to those who already like us.

Be generous today, and don't expect favours in return. Note that these verses are not about being walked over – cheek-turning and tunic-giving are actually ways of making your assailant think twice about their actions.

NOTES

87

HYPOCRITES

Make a list of the five things that annoy you most about the world.

Then, make a list of the five people that annoy you most and why.

Read **Luke 6:37-42.**

Then ask someone you trust to compile a list of the most annoying things about you. You may find this list, and the comparisons, illuminating.

Did you even do the third list? Are we always keener to criticise than to accept criticism? Do we truly believe we are better than others? (Answer that question honestly.) Or do we want to pretend that we are, to impress people? These are two very different roots that produce similarly hypocritical weeds. Like me, on receiving your own 'annoying' list back, you may well spring into defensive mode, and try to explain away the things listed there as misconceptions. Why do we loudly proclaim that 'Nobody's perfect', but when we have the specific evidence for that fact pointed out to us about our own lives, believe something different?

Jesus gives us a simple method here for setting ourselves straight. If at any time we are thinking or speaking critically about someone, we should use it as an opportunity to examine that same area in our own lives, and let God's light shine into it. That way we will also be able to 'see clearly' to help our sisters or brothers (without the filter that would make us spiritually blind to their problems anyway).

Current trends have enabled many of us to engage in intellectual snobbery gone mad, as we 'tsk tsk' at the shallowness of celebrity magazines and relationships, and despair over the latest group of lab rats rolled out on reality TV. The truth is we are exposed to this stuff so much that it is changing us, much as we would like to believe we somehow hover above it on another spiritual plane. Jesus says 'Can a blind man lead a blind man?' We know he can't, but it doesn't stop us following some of the blind men and women on TV more than we follow Jesus in the Bible. Because, to be honest, it's easier to feel good about yourself when you set your standards lower. And feeling all right is what life's all about, isn't it?

As www.despair.com puts it, are we simply 'increasing success, by lowering expectations'? Where our eyes are trained will decide our values.

Spend some time praying about any issues that have been triggered by these thoughts. Read and pray about your original lists in light of what you have discovered about yourself.

NOTES

PRAYING WITH PASSION

Luke 7:1-10

It's a humbling thing to get down on your knees and plead for mercy. This is especially true if you are a well-respected centurion. What prevents us from being on our knees praying for the healing of friends or relatives or enemies? Is it our pride? Is the fear of failure that infects so many areas of our lives creeping into our prayer life too?

Sometimes we end up playing God in our prayers, rather than simply being ourselves, which is what God desires. It's his job to be God, and our job to tell him where we're at. I have been amazed recently by the frustration and complaint inherent in many of the prayers of the great fathers of the faith in Genesis and Exodus. As I read, I am at times thinking, 'Steady on lad. That's a bit cheeky...' In fact Abraham's promise from God that his offspring will be as numerous as the stars in the sky comes as a response to his barbed complaint in Genesis 15:2-3: "O Sovereign Lord, what can you give me since I remain childless...You have given me no children; so a servant in my household will be my heir."

I feel as if I have become far too polite in my prayers – second guessing God, and trying to control the situation.

'Dear God, I know you're probably very busy with many situations all over the world at present, but it would be awfully kind of you to heal my friend, or maybe just let them know your comfort, or maybe just say hello. However I am aware of the many reasons why you may want to reveal your plan through the continuance of this difficult season. Amen.'

Blah, blah, blah.

What about, 'God, he has two kids under five and a wife who loves him dearly, so don't tell me this is a good time for him to get cancer. They're financially up the spout too, and you know that, so please do something before it's too late. Amen.'

Spend some time today on your knees praying for those that are unwell or in trouble. Be prepared to plead. Be prepared to cry and be prepared to be angry. Pray that Jesus will be as amazed by your passion and faith as he was that day with the centurion. It evokes a response, whether it is the one we desire or not.

NOTES

89

DISCUSSING DOUBTS

Make your way to a place which has some significance regarding your journey of learning to trust people or things. For me it is a swimming pool, as I was ten years old before I could trust the water and trust myself to go 10m without drowning. Sit down to read.

Luke 7:11-20

The verse where John asks, 'Are you the one who was to come, or should we expect someone else?' has always amazed me. John was the one who baptised Jesus after all (how could he forget something that was part of his name?) yet he sends his disciples to find out if Jesus really is the Messiah. John must either be suffering from amnesia or depression, or being incredibly fussy (well, yes the miracles were good, but I've seen better...). Perhaps he can't quite believe what he's got himself into, and is looking for an escape clause.

But as I start throwing stones, I realise that the funny thing is I've also met Jesus, and I've seen what He can do, yet there are times when I think 'Are we all just deluding ourselves?'

Many months before Thomas, John is holding out an empathetic fig leaf to all of us doubters. Throughout the Psalms David articulated his doubts to God. They weren't a comment on his relationship with God. They were an integral part of his relationship with God. We've all had conversations with friends where only when we've asked the awkward question has the conversation got down to the nitty-gritty. That is when we discover another layer or angle that we hadn't seen. Basically the relationship deepens. That is what can happen with God if we're honest about our doubts. The worst case scenario is that we suppress our doubts for years, and then when a traumatic life situation occurs which simply 'does not compute', we just lose it totally. Baby Jesus goes out with the bath water.

As John articulated his doubts, perhaps he discovered that they could be more accurately described as misunderstandings. You see 'Jesus the Liberator' hadn't liberated the Jews from the Romans as many were expecting and he was experiencing the sharp end of this, sitting frustratedly in prison. After the exchange, he was beginning to understand that the Kingdom of this Messiah was not coming in a purely political way, but that it was something much wider and deeper. John wouldn't have made this discovery, however, if he hadn't been honest in expressing his doubts and concerns.

In this place, take some time to talk through your doubts with God today.

NOTES ●✛

PART 1: LUKE

SEASON 3

90

FRUITFUL

Luke 7:21-35

If you could pick one phrase to sum up this passage of Scripture from start to finish, it would be, 'Look at the fruit!' Jesus is saying 'Don't just look at me, look at the fruit.' Verse 35 sums it all up when Jesus says 'wisdom is proved right by all her children.'

I always think that Jesus is incredibly gracious in his response to John's question. If it were me, I'd be thinking, 'Excuse me? What more do I have to do??? Don't you know who I am? (evidently not.)' Jesus instead lets his actions speak louder than words, and rather than scoff at John's lack of faith, he actually makes a point of praising him. This affirmation rises to the crescendo of verse 28, 'I tell you, among those born of women there is no-one greater than John; yet the one who is least in the Kingdom of God is greater than he.'

So in looking at your life, perhaps we should look at your fruit, not just at you. Go to your nearest fruit and vegetable store or supermarket, and spend some time looking around the fruit. Marvel at the different shapes and sizes, and the variety of countries they are from. Now put some fruit in your basket to represent a person or circumstance where your life has borne fruit. You may have invested heavily in one family member, so simply come out with one big juicy melon to be proud of. Or perhaps you're a teacher continually investing smaller amounts in many young people, so will enjoy munching your way through a bag of seedless grapes.

It's worth stopping at this point to think about how fruit is produced. A friend recently remarked to me that as a tree you can't make your fruit grow. Trees don't stand there intentionally squeezing their juices towards the tips of their branches, thinking 'grow, grow, go on, grow...' Their 'responsibility' is solely to make sure that they have their roots in the right place, and that they are receiving sunlight. Could the same be true for us? Are we sometimes so busy trying to 'make things happen' – to 'make the fruit grow', that we forget to keep our roots firmly in well-watered soil, cutting ourselves off from the only nourishment that can make it happen? Keith Green summed it up well in his song Rushing Wind, when he asked to be planted deep, by living waters, so that he could grow. Perhaps sometimes our only responsibility is to be in the right place, making sure that we are exposing ourselves to the light of his presence, planted in the soil of his word. Then the fruit will come naturally.

For the length of time that the fruits you purchased stay in your bowl or on your palate, let them be an real encouragement to you and encourage you to pray for these people or places. Next time you're back in that aisle, or near the fruit bowl, they will hopefully provide a visual hook to remind you to pray further for them.

NOTES

O.T.T.

Luke 7:36-50

For me, this story is a beautiful picture of unbridled worship. This woman does not care who else is in the room. She simply desires to pour all her love in the direction of this one man. The word used here for 'kiss' means 'to kiss fondly, to caress' or to 'kiss again and again.' The image of her wiping his feet with her tears is so beautiful that we forget that this means she must also have been crying in Jesus' presence. This is surely an appropriate response to the love that is forgiving her.

Where did we learn that we should suppress our emotions in worship? Certainly not in the Bible. How I long for this kind of freedom in worship. What a contrast to the Pharisees, who are doing everything by the book, but failing to show any real hospitality. Are we more concerned with what people around us will think, and what is 'proper', than giving our all to Jesus? The extravagance of his love to us demands an extravagant response. When was the last time you were extravagant in your love of God? When was the last time you really went over-the-top? Or are you inhibited by some Pharisees, or the Pharisee in yourself?

You have been forgiven much. None of us in this world have been forgiven 'little', so we don't have that as an opt-out clause.

Find a way to express your love to God extravagantly. This may be with a massive painting or sculpture, a really loud song, a long night on the dance floor with hands in the air, or a big donation to your church.

Now make plans to bless a brother or sister with an extravagant gift. Something that doesn't necessarily make any sense, either to your bank balance, or to your schedule, but something that will bless them beyond belief. This may be replacing a broken appliance, or buying them tickets to a concert, or flights to Paris. When did Jesus ever say 'Blessed are the measured'?

NOTES ●◆

92

DRIVING FORCE

Luke 8:1-3

Take a good look at the engine of your car (or any car, but ask permission first). You don't normally see it in action (hopefully) but it is essential to the car moving forward. In verses 1-3, we have some clues to the engine that was keeping the show on the road for Jesus and his disciples. I can only imagine all the wisdom, caring, tending, food-making etc., not to mention the fact that they actually footed many of the bills. Stop right now (perhaps as you rest on the car), and thank God for the folks who make up the engine of your life. Thank God for their sacrifice on your behalf. It was a large sacrifice for the biblical women, and not only financially. For women to be travelling with a group of men in those times would have had a major impact on their social standing and reputation.

Later on, thank the people who make up 'your engine' personally.

NOTES

93

SCATTER THE SEED

Luke 8:4-15

Scatter some seeds in four different parts of your garden, or an area in the vicinity of where you live. Find a path, some rocks, some weeds, and some good soil. As you do so, pray for the people in your life that fall into the four categories as described by Jesus.

Ask him if he is calling you to cultivate some of the poor soil of your friends' lives, perhaps by removing some rocks, pointing out some weeds, breaking up the cement, or irrigating the ground with some encouragement.

The rocks could be things like unhealthy relationships with the opposite sex, which prevent anyone getting close. The weeds could be bad habits that seem to grow as they grow, stealing precious nutrition. Sometimes it will require an initial thump to break up the ground, but always speak the truth in love.

Check back to see how they are doing in a few weeks.

NOTES

BLINDING LIGHT

Stare at a lampshade that is hiding a light-bulb. Now stare at the light-bulb with the shade removed (or simply change angle). Are you seeing strange patterns in front of your eyes? Light that is allowed to shine has a profound effect.

If you can, now read **Luke 8:16-18.**

Are people blinded by you, or just mildly better illuminated? Is your light out in the open for all to see, or just a pocket torch for personal use to sort yourself out in emergencies?

'No-one lights a lamp and hides it in a jar or puts it under a bed. Instead, he puts it on a stand, so that those who come in can see the light.'

At night-time, take a walk down your street and make a mental note of which houses you are naturally drawn to. My guess is that there will be a common factor – their lights are on. There is something welcoming about light, but these days, we often put coloured gels over our light to make it more appealing to others, in case the brightness scares them away. Lighting engineers use gels to prevent dazzling the performers on a stage. Are there any ways in which you are colouring the bright white light of God?

In the future, as you switch lights on and off in your house, let it be a reminder to pray that your light would be undimmed and visible for all to see.

NOTES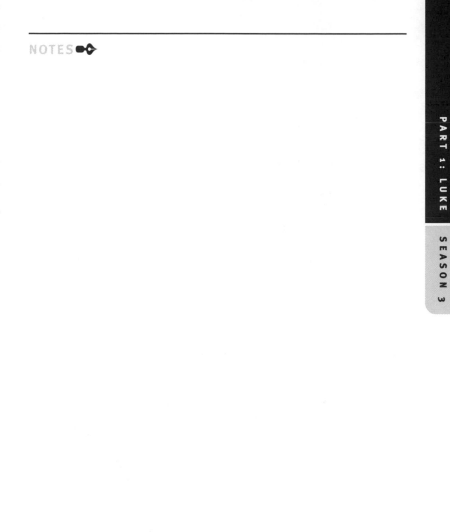

95

STORMY WEATHER

Do this devotional in your car (but not while driving).

Read **Luke 8:22-25**.

I think if Jesus had asked me 'Where is your faith?' during this episode, I'd have been tempted to shout, 'In the same place as my guts' or words to that effect. We need no convincing – with tsunamis in the Far East and tornadoes in Birmingham – weather is pretty powerful stuff. It is perhaps one of the few things which we feel 'happens' to us – something we have no control over. So our amazement would be similar to the disciples at this man who the winds and waves obeyed. Jesus not only calms the storm, he is the calm in the storm. In the midst of their lack of faith, we forget that the disciples played a vital role in this incident. They did wake him. They did know where to go for help.

What are the storms in your life? What circumstances brew up quickly, scare the life out of you, bring nausea, cause you to cling on to anything, but disappear sometimes as quickly as they came? If you're in a storm, don't hide away. Be honest, and tell him that you fear you're about to drown.

Write down what you're going to tell Jesus, once you've woken him up.

A common modern-day storm is the one that erupts when people are stuck in heavy traffic. The dark clouds descend right into the car, and the slightest provocation results in thunder and sometimes lightning. Do you rouse Jesus who is sleeping in the passenger seat, or are you too embarrassed? Will you give him the chance to bring his calm and peace?

Pray for an awareness of his presence in your driving life and other 'stormy' situations. Let this experience be a reminder the next time you see the dark clouds approaching!

NOTES ✏️

96

SNAIL-S-PACE

Luke 8:40-56

Do you remember Jesus rushing anywhere? It would have provided great drama for the Gospel writers, so I suspect if it had happened, they wouldn't have been able to resist including it. I can't find even one example. Even in this desperate situation, when a man is about to lose his only daughter, Jesus is unflappable. This is 'the peace of Christ' that is also available to us. It must have an impact on the physical as well as the spiritual. It defines a way of living as a human being with a sense of the divine.

See if you can get to the bottom of why you rush around in life. Many of us tell little lies to each other in this area. How long will you be? 'About ten minutes', when perhaps a more sober judgement would be twenty-five. We undervalue other people and we put ourselves under pressure with this sort of behaviour. It's not efficiency. It's very slow spiritual suicide. It's hard not to pick up the 'rushing' vibes from those around us in the street or in places like the London underground. We suddenly find ourselves walking fast, or running, before we realise that we aren't in a rush.

Like me, do you boot up your computer before doing anything else when you walk into a room, giving you about a minute to do other useful things? Do you start to boil the kettle before anything else in the kitchen, as it may be the limiting factor of a cooking process? Multi-tasking can be useful, but it has turned efficiency into a god. If you trace back the reasons for many of our decisions they go back to the big 'e' of efficiency.

I made a liberating discovery about four years ago. Walking: I just walked. I stopped running. (And I don't just mean on my feet. I mean walking in my head.) The earth-shattering discovery was this. I was actually experiencing a moment, rather than simply planning the next moment, and in that space I knew God with me. Previously I had been so preoccupied making sure that the next moments happened efficiently, I could get to the end of a day and not really have experienced any of it. Stop for a second right now to recognise Immanuel – 'God with us'.

If it isn't God asking us to cram so much into our lives, then who is it? And why are we listening? Intentionally take longer to perform various tasks today, and enjoy the space in your head and heart that this provides. Savour things, don't use them.

If you'd like to explore some more about where our crazy pace of life has sprung from, (and ways to slow it down), I'd recommend the book In Praise of Slow[10] by Carl Honore. It challenged me a lot.

NOTES ●◆

LET YES MEAN YES

Luke 8:26-39

Here Jesus answers two questions in radically different ways in the space of a couple of verses (verses 37 and 39). The people are scared and ask him to leave. He says yes. God never forces his way into a life. The previously demon-possessed man begs to go with Jesus. He says no. There is a time for spending intense solo time with Jesus and a time for sharing his story.

I don't know about you but I struggle with yes and no these days. They are so definite and don't leave options open. I am more likely to say 'maybe' or 'potentially'. Something about 'letting your Yes be a Yes' springs to mind. Is it our fear of making the wrong decision or of missing out on opportunities? Only by making decisions and seeing the consequences do we learn. Or we could just float on in a sea of vagueness. Often we are scared of offending people with a 'No'. We need that same confidence in our overall priorities that Jesus had from his close communication with his Father.

Are there areas of your life in which you are procrastinating at present? Is it time for a decision about a relationship, job, location or church? Count the number of yes/no decisions that you make today.

Stick two sheets on your wall. A big red NO sheet, and a big green YES sheet. As time passes by, bring your choices to God and to help you concrete your choice, place it or write it on the appropriate sheet. You may see a pattern start to emerge, where God is revealing what and where he is calling you to, and what is he not calling you to. Believing that it is all right not to be called is sometimes harder than the other way around.

I have found this meditation very helpful:

Our work in creation

I have not lost my way – it is just that so many ways open before me that sometimes I hardly know which way to choose. To decide for one is to decide against another. I never imagined it would be this hard. Now you know. The higher a person's call or vision, the more choices are given them. This is our work in creation: to decide. And what we decide is woven into the thread of time and being forever. Choose wisely then, but you must choose.

– Stephen Lawhead, Merlin [11]

NOTES ●◆

98

EXPERIENCE ADVENTURE

Luke 9:1-6

I'm wondering more and more if we miss out on discovering the best of ourselves and each other in relationships because we have lost a sense of adventure. Some of the most bonding moments in my life have occurred when myself and other folks have had to work together in awkward circumstances to complete some sort of mission. If I made an honest observation of my own life and my older friends' lives over the last few years, it would be that often we are actually going out of our way to avoid awkward situations, and therefore avoid challenges. This may be in the realm of conversation, sport, the area of a town you live in or any situation where we have learnt to 'manage' the random variables to enable us to lead a settled, 'normal' life. This is not the sort of life I see Jesus or his disciples living in the Gospels. He was constantly taking risky, low-security decisions.

Is there a challenge that you and some friends could embark on, that might by its nature require some ingenuity, some prayer, some faith, and cause you to depend on each other, rather than stay wrapped up in self-sufficiency? Or will the closest you get to the words 'unexpected', 'spontaneous' and 'scary' be a day at Alton Towers? The place of stretching is the place where we grow.

Here are some ideas to get your thoughts going – climbing a mountain, fostering a child, selling up and moving to a cheaper part of town, staging a musical, starting a small business, building a school/hospital in Africa, preaching in Russia.

The disciples had to have faith when Jesus sent them out, because it was all they had. Is our lack of faith in seeing God move directly dependent on our lack of need? A wise man once said 'With Jesus, you don't know what you have, until he is all you have.' Jesus gives us the same authority and the same command that he gave to those disciples. Why aren't we out there?

NOTES

99

WIRED FOR SOUND

Luke 9:51-56 and **13:31-35**.

Do you remember the frantic discussions after the first U.S. presidential debate of 2004? George Bush had seemed more stilted than normal, and then some eagle-eyed reporter spotted a strange bulge in the President's jacket in a photo. Commentators had a field-day suggesting that he was being prompted by an advisor via an earpiece.

It made me think about how Jesus acted during his life. It always seemed as if he was hearing instructions from somewhere else. He could see the big picture, when all those around him could only see the obvious.

I worry about what I'm wired to. It's becoming harder rather than easier. Twenty-four hour news media and the Internet means that we now feel a need to check up what is going on in the world at regular intervals. The problem is that the more I am wired to this stuff, the less my head and heart have space to be wired to my Father, as Jesus was. Add to that the near hard-wiring of our iPods and MP3 players, which block out much human interaction, never mind divine interaction, and you begin to worry whether we'll ever hear God again. Obviously I'm not saying that God can't communicate with us through music etc., but it's all a question of priorities.

Bear with me on this one. If you have a personal stereo or an iPod that you use regularly, then wire yourself up and go for a walk. But don't switch it on. It will help plant this 'wiring' thought in your brain, for future living and listening. Listen to the silence. Pray for God to direct you as he directed Jesus. Pray for the development of an intimacy which will lead to a simple knowing of the Father's heart in any given situation. And smile because you know something that the people walking past you don't.

NOTES ✒

SEASON 3

PART 2

100

BIN IT TO WIN IT

Matthew 6:25-34

In this passage I hear echoes of Jesus' beautiful words to Martha in Luke 10:41-42, 'Martha, Martha,' the Lord answered, 'you are worried and upset about many things, but only one thing is needed. Mary has chosen what is better, and it will not be taken away from her.'

In Matthew 6 Jesus is simply listing the 'many things' that we worry about. Later in the chapter we find out what the 'one thing' that we should be worried about is. (I'm realising how ironic it is that I just used that phrase. In our speech patterns, we have actually normalised worrying.) The 'one thing' is to 'seek first his Kingdom and his righteousness, and all these things will be given to you as well.'

There is a real power in simply listing your worries. By naming them you remove the subconscious power from them. Write them on a piece of paper and then go out for a walk. Don't throw the paper into the nearest bin. Instead take some time to lay these worries before God honestly, one at a time, and when you know that the time is right, just dump them in a roadside bin. They will be far from your house and you can experience the difference during your walk home, knowing that God has heard you and that you've been obedient to his command 'Do not worry about your life.'

In the same way that 'peace is not simply the absence of war', you could also say that 'peace is not simply the absence of worry.'

Colossians 3:15
> Let the peace of Christ rule in your hearts, since as members of one body you were called to peace. And be thankful.

When do we truly let peace 'rule'? I think I'm happy to let peace in as a passenger every so often, when I need it, but what would my life look like if I let it drive? No more worrying about the speed cameras and short-sighted pedestrians of my emotional and spiritual world. Peace just slips down a gear and smiles reassuringly that he knows where he's going and that we'll make it on time.

Don't worry.

NOTES

PART 2

SEASON 3

GOD'S TAKE

Read 2 Kings 22

I have started asking the interesting question, 'How are you, God?' I not only want to know the truth about God's character and his attributes displayed through history. I want to know what he feels about situations now. I want to know what he is laughing at, what he is crying at, and what he is raging about. I know most of those things are probably going on all at once, but to feel and see just a snapshot of them in the midst of my daily life is surely vital if I am to truly be his hands and his feet.

As Christians we're so good at declaring God's opinion on every subject. We bust a gut to dot all the i's and cross all the t's to make sure we know precisely the right answer in every situation, and we will take those to task who may disagree with us. But I wonder if we shouldn't be spending a greater amount of time asking God what his priorities are for us and our nations.

For example, in my homeland of Northern Ireland, I am convinced that at the moment one of God's top priorities is to see two sides of a divided community reconciled. His heart beats for it so loudly. But observing fractured church life, you could be forgiven for drawing the conclusion that staying doctrinally pure to avoid any theological risk was top priority. Is Jesus shouting more about Jerry Springer the Opera, or global economic injustice right now? I have my suspicions. However, if you are going to seek God's heart, be prepared for it to burst open. Then you may well be able to respond like King Josiah, as mentioned in verse 19.

2 Kings 22:19
> Because your heart was responsive and you humbled yourself before the Lord when you heard what I have spoken against this place and its people, that they would become accursed and laid waste, and because you tore your robes and wept in my presence, I have heard you, declares the Lord.

Do you ever feel that you aren't experiencing life at full volume? That you stay slightly detached to protect your heart? God could have done that. He didn't. Ask God to show you his heart emotions towards various situations in your life, the lives of your friends and the world at large.

After prayer make a list of what you think God's top three priorities are for
- the world
- your town
- your life
at this moment in time.

Ask him, 'How are you?', and get used to asking it.

NOTES

102

TOMORROW'S HEADLINES

Take a pen, some paper and a Bible. Find a disused piece of wasteland in your area.

Sit down and read **Ezekiel 37:1-14**.

Prophecy is about speaking God's truth into situations right now, not just second guessing the future. It is about seeing the unseen, and sometimes by your very words or actions being part of bringing it into being. For Ezekiel, it required faith to see potential life in the midst of 'Death valley', and any prophet always runs the risk of being left standing, looking stupid, with nothing happening. It can be a lonely place. All of which sometimes prevents us from stepping out and speaking what we believe God gives us to speak, or what we know is on God's heart. As with any spiritual discipline or gifting, you can't wait to be perfect before you start using it, so here's an experience to help.

Imagine what this land could become. Imagine what it could provide. Imagine what facilities could be available. Imagine what resources could be distributed from here. Imagine what impact it could have on the surrounding area. Let your praying passion roam free. Write or draw what could come to pass.

When you get back....

Write down five headlines that you would like to see on the front page of The Times, or on the BBC News website tomorrow morning. Cast your net wide. Speak into areas of health, education, politics, sport, the environment etc.

See the 'as yet unseen.' Pray for it to be so.

NOTES

SETTING THE SCENE

Another great way of bringing Bible stories to life is by reading them in a context similar to the story. There are many obvious examples of this.

- stories of the fishermen – sitting by a harbour
- scenes from the centre of Jerusalem – sitting in a crowded city centre
- the Christmas story – sitting in a hotel lobby
- wanderings in the desert – the most deserted place you can find
- the garden of Eden – out in your garden (surprise, surprise)

Often something from a passage will come to life purely because you are outside. I will never forget reading about Jesus' temptation by Satan to throw himself from that high point while I was standing on the top of a cliff. You will remember much more of what you read, because there is a 'time and place' memory attached to it. The things you see may well also bring added depth and understanding to the imagery of the story. For example, I remember being struck by the chaos, innocence and enthusiasm of primary school children running around a playground as I walked past a school one day. I stopped to read Mark 10:15

> 'I tell you the truth, anyone who will not receive the Kingdom of God like a little child will never enter it.'

I had been given a deeper insight into what it would look like for me to be truly childlike before my God.

To get you started, head to your nearest main road and sit (safely) nearby and read Jeremiah chapter 31. At times, you may also want to walk and pray the words. Let it lead you into prayers for your own journey.

There is an interesting point here with regard to the 'road signs' of verse 21. They refer to the piles of stones that people would leave in the desert while on their way somewhere, so they could find their way back. The 'away' journey here refers to the children of Israel being taken into captivity in Assyria. Even if we know that we are heading to a 'season of exile' in our lives, do we make sure that we leave some signposts so that we can find our way back? For instance, do we cut off ties with those who we know will call us to account? Are we honest with people, so they can understand our journey, or do we let our 'misunderstoodness' become another reason for staying away?

NOTES

MUNCH LUNCH

John 21:1-14

Jesus knew the value of bringing people together to eat, whether it was kippers for breakfast on the beach, a 'leaving-do' in an upper room, or a ready-meal for five (thousand). When the disciples suggested dispersing a crowd to let them fend for themselves, Jesus' natural instinct was to keep them together.

Could you organise a barbeque or a picnic for the people that live in your immediate neighbourhood? It may involve a bit of travel, or it may simply be on the grass in front of your houses, or in a nearby park. So often, we twist our minds trying to find common ground on which to connect with folks who aren't yet believers. Perhaps the answer is simpler. Eating is probably the most common ground you can find. We all know how to do it, and in its preparation we will find the bonding of a task carried out on a level playing field.

Don't fall into that classic Christian trap of making it into an 'event.' Amazingly, the early church grew without posters. Just do it as a human being, inviting other human beings to eat with you. Sharing your life with someone often starts by sharing food with them.

Pray for wisdom and courage in building social contexts which mix believers and 'not-yet' believers. Don't succumb to the laziness of compartmentalising your life.

NOTES

105

GET OUT

Matthew 8:20

> Jesus replied, "Foxes have holes and birds of the air have nests, but the Son of Man has nowhere to lay his head."

If it's not totally irresponsible to those close to you, sleep rough tonight. Discover what it is like to be homeless, even for just one night. You may want to do this with a friend or two. You will learn more and perhaps your heart will be softened more in eight hours than in a month of seminars on the subject. The cold, the loneliness and the vulnerability are merely concepts until you experience them.

On an earthly level, you could describe Jesus as homeless, but he was also displaced from his real home with his Father. Again Jesus shows his identification with those on the fringes of society. Tonight you are identifying with millions of displaced people across our world who for various reasons have no roof over their heads, whether it is refugees from war in sub-Saharan Africa, street children in Central America, or the folks in your own town whose stories you only half believe.

Spend your sleepless moments praying for these situations. You may also want to identify with another sleepless night of prayer – that of Jesus in the Garden of Gethsemane. He may ask us, 'Could you watch and pray with me for but a few hours to kneel alongside the broken and dispossessed of my world?'

NOTES

106

PEOPLE OF LIGHT

Tonight, turn off the lights in your house for one hour and attempt to perform all your normal tasks. With the 'leaders of the earth' of Job 12 you may well 'grope in darkness with no light'. (Disclaimer – the author is not liable for any injuries caused.) Do we simply take 'living in the light' for granted? Just experience sitting in the dark for some time. How does it make you feel?

Light a single candle and read from **1 Peter 2:9-12**, which includes

> But you are a chosen people, a royal priesthood, a holy nation, a people belonging to God, that you may declare the praises of him who called you out of darkness into his wonderful light.

Take at least fifteen minutes to simply worship God in speech or song after meditating on those wonderful verses. Worship is the reason for our existence as people of the light. Look at verse 9 – we are chosen and called to the light that we may declare his praises.... It's our raison d'etre. Thank him that we no longer have to sit or operate in the darkness. We can truly see. Thank him for all the things in your life that you now see, which you were blind to while in the darkness. The website also has a presentation of verses on this theme that you could watch in the dark.

Turn the lights back on.

NOTES

107

GET REAL

When David wrote his Psalms, they spoke of all the real world battles, frustrations and failures that he was experiencing at that moment. They were an honest expression of his prevailing mood and attitude towards God. I suspect David would be more than slightly confused to wander into our churches and find us mostly singing and saying words that someone else has written, not words that are springing from our own hearts and minds. Of course, the psalter and other liturgies are essential texts that provide a biblical framework for our worship, but it is again a matter of balance. How do we truly know how people are doing, if they only ever sing the words we tell them to?

Pick any one of the Psalms and read it now. Let its reality release your own honesty toward God. Then set your Bible down, lift a pen or pull your keyboard towards you and write your own psalm of praise. Use the language and imagery of now, as David did. (When was the last time you ran away from soldiers into a 'strong tower'?) Go through the pain barrier of using non 'worship-bubble' words in worship. Here is an example when I tried. (It happened to be a happy day!)

> This is great Lord
> This life just gets better and better.
> Not easier, but better and better.
> But I want to get better and better too.
>
> I think I see two modes to my life, Lord;
> Seeking and stumbling.
> And I know that I learn from the falling, but would you help me spot the tripwires?
> Give me your infra-red vision to spot those red lasers of temptation.

I'll be more honest with you and my mates – more current with you – more Five Live and less Daily Telegraph.

I want lots of short Internet accounts with you, not one big TESSA that I never touch.

You do know best, and I love the fact that as well as crying when I stumble, there is a part of you that laughs. Thank you that you don't take me as seriously as I do.

Please explode into my consciousness with such volume, or with such silence that I can't ignore you. Sorry that you often have to strain your voice over the background noise, and even then you still take 'no' for answer.

I may run away, but still the dynamic duo of Goodness and Mercy will chase after me like Starsky and Hutch...

....all the days of my life.

Help me hear the sirens.

___

NOTES

LITERARY REVIEW

How much do you read? In the instant world of 24-hour news media and celebrity magazines, do you give yourself the space to enjoy a good book? Is there a pile of them in your bookcase waiting to be devoured? If so, start one today, or visit your local library. It's still free, and they have to order whichever book you ask them to, even Christian ones. This can also be done through your library's website and may have the knock-on effect of bumping up the percentage of Christian books that the average browser may stumble upon.

Now how much do you read the book? Or more accurately the books, as that is what Bible means. Tot up the number of these books you have read in the past month. Be honest with yourself.

Mark 12:26

> Now about the dead rising—have you not read in the book of Moses, in the account of the bush, how God said to him, 'I am the God of Abraham, the God of Isaac, and the God of Jacob'?

This is one Jesus' favourite forms of speech. There are six separate instances recorded in the Gospels of him saying 'Have you not read…?' There is an inherent frustration in the phrase. You can imagine it bubbling up. What? They don't know this either? If they knew all the effort we'd put in to make sure that the truth was passed on accurately. And they can't even be bothered to read it.

It was all there. The prophecies about Jesus. Their role as a light for the Gentiles. It was all there. Yet the Jews missed it.

All we need to know is also all there in the Bible. Our status as beloved sons and daughters. The happy ending. His desire to work with us. Yet so often we miss it too. Not because we don't like the Bible or disagree with it, but simply because it's been a while since we were near it.

Learning by your mistakes still works, but avoiding them lets you learn and grow more quickly, without hurting as many others and yourself in the process. Engaging with the Bible regularly is a key part of this. You'd be amazed how much of the Bible you can read if you set aside time to do it. Audio CDs are now readily available, for those of you who spend a lot of your lives in the car, or struggle to read. You can get through the New Testament in a return trip from London to Edinburgh. I bought the NIV audio CD version for one of the guys I mentor a few months ago, and he straight away put it all on his iPod for his morning commute to London.

Read 'the books'.

NOTES

POSITIVE POST

Read **3 John**. It is a little gem of a letter towards the end of the New Testament that is easy to pass over. If I were Gaius, the recipient of this letter, I think my mood would lift considerably as I read about my own 'faithfulness to the truth.'

Hopefully you have experienced the joy of receiving an unexpected letter. It may have been from someone you haven't seen in a long time, or from someone you see all the time, but the content and the fact that they took the time to write makes it very significant. There is something about putting pen to paper that commits us to thoughts and words of encouragement, making them more meaningful and permanent for people. I secretly stash many of the amazing letters that have encouraged me during my life.

Ask God to point you in the direction of someone who could do with this form of solid encouragement. (You probably already know who it could be.)

Then get writing.

NOTES

THESE FEET WERE MADE FOR WALKING

Romans 1:20

> For since the creation of the world, God's invisible qualities—his eternal power and divine nature—have been clearly seen, being understood from what has been made, so that men are without excuse.

Simply take some time to enjoy nature, and thereby understand more of God's 'invisible qualities'. You may want to take a camera or a note-book to note down what you learn about the character of God.

I have discovered one of the keys to enjoying the beauty that God has created around me – walking. When I drive to places, I miss so much: for instance the amazing leaves on the tree just up the road from my house or the squirrels scurrying around behind no. 28's hedge. When you're walking, you have time to appreciate the formation of the clouds, the variety of other people's faces and voices, and the sounds of birds. You don't need to drive to a forest park. (But feel free.) Just walk.

While outside or on your return, read Psalm 8 as an act of worship.

NOTES

BLOOD TEST

Psalm 106:6

> We have sinned, even as our fathers did;
> we have done wrong and acted wickedly.

Whether we like it or not, our parents have a massive influence on who we are. We are quite literally made of the 'same stuff'. Some of the most releasing and profitable times in my friends' lives have been those times when they sat down and realised where the echoes of their parents were in their lives, both positive and negative. This can truly be an 'Aha!' moment. It's one of the few methods we have for understanding ourselves and cutting ourselves a bit of slack.

This is not a place for blaming or finger-pointing, but honest evaluation of the strengths and weaknesses of your bloodlines. Remember our parents were only working from the cards that they themselves were dealt. Sometimes we directly inherit things, sometimes our rebellion to a certain aspect of our upbringing resides for longer than we think, and sometimes just being in the environment of certain stuff makes it hard to escape it.

So take some time to think about making the most of the good that has been handed down to you, and avoiding the same mistakes as your ancestors.

> Slowly think through headings like these;
> – attitudes to money
> – attitudes to the opposite sex
> – desire to control
> – attitudes to long-term commitment
> – attitudes to other family members
> – competition

- hospitality
- 'what will the neighbours think?' syndrome
- style of communication
- volume levels of communication
- pornography
- insecurity

If you feel it's appropriate, you may want to discuss some of these things with your siblings.

Ask a close friend to pray with you about what you have discovered. If you need to repent or let go of some things, then this is the time.

NOTES

TRUE LIES

John 1:14

The Word became flesh and made his dwelling among us. We have seen his glory, the glory of the One and Only, who came from the Father, full of grace and truth.

Today a poem to meditate on:

You said that you were the truth
Not that you spoke it, but that you were it.
Help me wear it.

John said that you were 'full of grace and truth'
But we've jumped straight to the main course.
Help me taste your starter of grace.

I've been checking you out.
Re-reading your stories.
Your words came wrapped in love.

If you are the truth,
Then I can speak words in a way
That correctly exposes the facts,
But misses the truth.

Perhaps the words even cease to be true.

Sometimes I want to be right
More than
I want to be you.

A Flannagan

Jesus said 'I am the truth'. Truth is found in a person, and a person is much more than a set of vital statistics and facts. Jesus embodies truth. So are there times when we communicate correct facts, but fail to show 'the truth' because the way we articulate them falls outside the way that Jesus would have done it?

Skim read through any three chapters of Matthew's Gospel today noting not the content of what Jesus says, but the manner and context in which he speaks (or declines to). A Bible where his words are in red will help.

Make a list of what you notice, for application and prayer into your own life.

P A R T 2

NOTES ●◆

S E A S O N 3

113

WATCH OUT

Psalm 39:5

> You have made my days a mere handbreadth;
> the span of my years is as nothing before you.
> Each man's life is but a breath.

Psalm 90:4

> For a thousand years in your sight
> are like a day that has just gone by,
> or like a watch in the night.

Last summer I had a wonderful time with a lovely couple. They provided me with a bed, some food and some prayers. They had a beautiful peace and calm about their lives. As I was leaving, the grandfather clock chimed 8 o'clock and, looking up at it, I was surprised to see that the minute hand was missing. After I had commented on the missing hand, my host corrected me, explaining that the clock was two hundred years old, and that was how many clocks were made in those days. 'It's perfect for us', he said. 'We don't need a minute hand. We're in the country here.' What an amazing metaphor for the calm unhurriedness that I craved in my life and that I had observed in this couple.

Could we remove the minute hand from our watches or clocks? Plan a day in the near future when you will leave your watch at home, or if you really need it, at least hidden in a nearby drawer. Experience the joys of not being a slave to time for just one day. Make judgements based on people and relationships rather than deadlines and schedules.

After doing this for one day, I kept doing it, and now haven't worn a watch for seven months. It's amazing how you still get to places on time, but you aren't ruled by time. Okay, so I do have a mobile in my pocket to help, but I can honestly say this has slowed me down for the better, and I hope my friends would testify to that.

Spend some time praying for a sense of God's perfect timing. Meditate on the verses above and accept that God's timing is often not the same as our timing. I will never get done all the things that I would like to get done but sometimes my actions betray that truth. Sometimes the things or people I trample on to get them done negates the good that I am trying to do.

NOTES

EXERCISING FAITH

1 Timothy 4:1-8

I don't know if you're the sort of person who is meant to stretch every morning, for example to help your back, neck or shoulders. If you're like me, you often feel a bit guilty for not doing your stretches, and if you've also got guilt because you haven't spent time with God, then this exercise could be for you. I'm walking very gingerly here (not because of a bad back), but because I don't want to fall into the territory of 'Praise Aerobics' videos!

It is actually quite a natural fit. Stretches work best when you take some time over them and do them very slowly. In fact they can be counter-productive if rushed. The same could be said of prayer. The concept is simple. While you're stretching, ask for God to stretch you in the different areas of your life. Pray for the faith to occasionally sprint, taking risks and trusting his provision. Pray for the infilling of his Spirit to power your spiritual muscles. In the same way that an athlete's muscles do not function to their full potential unless they have been stretched, neither do our spiritual muscles ever see their full potential unless we are in situations which stretch us. This is why Paul intentionally uses the word 'training' to describe how Timothy should develop – 'train yourself to be godly.'

Praying verses of Scripture repeatedly can be helpful here. For example:

Zechariah 4:6
'Not by might nor by power, but by my Spirit,' says the Lord Almighty.

You could build a routine using different topics, whereby you pray for your job environment when stretching your neck muscles, your family environment when stretching your back etc. etc.

NOTES

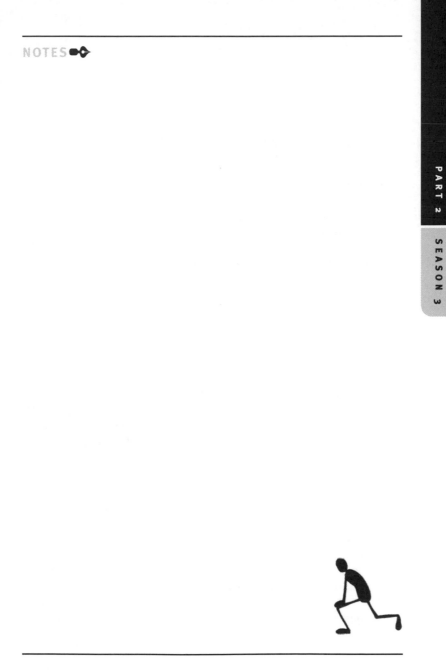

BRAND NEW

Isaiah 45:18

> For this is what the Lord says—
> he who created the heavens,
> he is God;
> he who fashioned and made the earth,
> he founded it;
> he did not create it to be empty,
> but formed it to be inhabited—
> he says:
> "I am the Lord
> and there is no other."

Can you believe that someone invented bungee jumping? Yes, before it became commonplace, someone tried it for the first time. Crazy, yes, risky, yes, but creative, yes! Everything in your life that you now take for granted was at once stage a crazy, risky experiment (or accident) – the light-bulb, the car, penicillin, ice cream, bridges.

A great definition of creativity is simply 'Bringing into being something that has never existed before.' We all have the image of our endlessly creative Creator within us. What is stopping you from 'seeing the unseen', and bringing things into being that have never existed before? We can too easily buy into the lie that creativity begins and ends with arty or musical types of people, leading to the popular excuse, 'Oh, I'm not creative.' It's simply that God's creativity will be expressed in different ways in different people (how creative). It's about 'newness', and a new plan for information flow in an office is just as new as a new song, and probably much harder work.

We are now so over-stimulated by every form of media that we don't have the need or space for creative thought. Emails are another example. I, like many of my peers find it much easier to answer twenty emails, being reactive, than to actually create the article, report or plan that I am putting off. Robbie Williams said 'Let me entertain you' and we sat down and said 'Okay then.' Some of us are yet to get off the couch.

So whatever your particular forte is, see what newness there may be lurking inside waiting to jump out. Create something today. It may seem unusual or a bit crazy, but remember that's often how anything of worth begins.

Pray that more and more of the Creator's creative energy would flow through your heart and mind. Pray that through this you would bring new life and light to people's lives.

NOTES

UNDER FIRE

I always enjoy watching (but not participating in) the discussion that goes something like this. **'You're a bit defensive, aren't you?' 'No, I'm not.'** 'There you go, you're doing it again.' 'D'oh!' Being labelled defensive seems to be an automatic negative, but you could argue that in terms of human interaction these days, we actually need a lot more defence and a lot less offence. Sometimes the problem in defensive reactions is not so much the word 'defensive' but the word 'reactions'.

When we ask the question 'What would Jesus do?' it's often not too hard to work out the answer, as we are calmly discussing a premeditated action. But where the wheels can come off is when we don't have time to work out the answer to the question 'How would Jesus react?' before we have reacted in a way that he probably wouldn't.

Organise to spend time with one (or a group) of your closest friends. Ask them the following sort of questions

- What are my defensive reactions?
- What statements or situations do I react badly to?
- How does that affect them?
- How could I improve?

What you'll find is that if you pray for each other and speak the truth in love, you could be the stimulus for everyone discussing their 'reactionary' lives and their reasons for them.

Sometimes we just need to learn to breathe before speaking or reacting, but sometimes we need to acknowledge the root of the reaction. What underground fear or false belief about ourselves or our relationship with this person is being triggered?

Throughout Luke 20, Jesus' authority and identity come under constant attack. Read it and let him teach you how to react.

NOTES

117

JUST PRAYERS

Buy a national newspaper today, and pray a half-minute prayer after reading every page. The state of our world means I suspect you will need no more inspiration than that.

Romans 8:26

> In the same way, the Spirit helps us in our weakness. We do not know what we ought to pray for, but the Spirit himself intercedes for us with groans that words cannot express.

Pray not just for the situations and the people, but the underlying causes and problems. All through the Old Testament, the foundations of God's rule are justice and righteousness. Pray for these good foundations to be rebuilt into the systems and structures of our society.

Isaiah 9:7

> Of the increase of his government and peace
> there will be no end.
> He will reign on David's throne
> and over his Kingdom,
> establishing and upholding it
> with justice and righteousness
> from that time on and for ever.
> The zeal of the Lord Almighty
> will accomplish this.

Pray specifically against any dark powers that are coming to bear on the situations you come across, for example spirits of hatred and racism, deception, or perverted sexuality.

Ephesians. 6:12

> For our struggle is not against flesh and blood, but against the rulers, against the authorities, against the powers of this dark world and against the spiritual forces of evil in the heavenly realms.

Hopefully this won't be the last time that your newspaper inspires some prayer.

NOTES

118

OPEN UP

Why do we close our eyes when we pray?

I know there are some practical reasons why sometimes it may be helpful, such as eliminating distractions, but the religious fervour with which we close our eyes on almost all occasions could make one believe that it is a prerequisite for prayer. There is no passage to read from the Bible today, because there is not even a phrase in the Old or New Testament which encourages us to close our eyes for prayer. (Unless you count something like 'Fix your eyes upon Jesus', which following literally would mean you'd cause quite a few road accidents.)

Closing your eyes for prayer can be a real barrier to deepening spiritual intimacy amongst groups of Christians. Like many other things it is an example of faith becoming privatised, leaving us safe to sit in our own little worlds, never ever having to 'share' our relationship with God by eye contact, while we're talking or listening to him. Time after time, I have seen the honesty level and spiritual depth of my relationships with people shoot upwards once we have gone through this pain barrier of making eye contact. What are we embarrassed about?

There is also a problem in that in terms of our mental framework, closing your eyes keeps God in heaven or 'someplace else'. The unspoken message is that we have to cease our physical existence for a moment to get him to answer the 'Spirit-phone'. Keeping your eyes open acknowledges that God is actually present wherever we are, by his Spirit. It helps to smash the false distinction between sacred and secular, or spiritual and physical.

To be honest, the closing of our eyes and squeezing of our minds to conjure up God could be described as closer to thought projection and various 'New Age' teachings than Christianity. I'm not saying that it's 'wrong' per se, but that we need some balance between open and closed.

Why not have a meal today with your 'family' where you pray and talk throughout the meal, with your eyes open, talking to God as if he was another person sitting around the table, because he is present.

NOTES ✒

119

DON'T POKE THE ROCK

Numbers 20:1-12

This story both amazes and scares me. The Children of Israel are complaining again – and again it's because of extreme thirst. For the umpteenth time Moses and Aaron get on their faces on their behalf before God and ask him to do something. On my first reading of this, I thought – great – water comes from the rock – God has moved – everyone's happy. But no. This is the horrendous moment where God declares that Moses and Aaron will not enter the Promised Land, because they didn't honour him as holy. I thought hang on, what went wrong? See if you can spot it.

Look closely at verse 8. What exactly did God instruct them to do? Instead Moses decided to turn the event into a David Copperfield-esque spectacle, with his magic staff. God's judgement seems especially harsh, since just three chapters earlier, this is exactly what Moses had done correctly. But just doing what we always do, and what we know works may not always be what God has in mind. Our desire should always be to glorify him, rather than simply doing what is practical.

This challenges me to my core. There are so many situations where I need to simply call out to God, but I just can't resist poking the rock. I can't stop myself making that extra phone call, or sending that text message to make sure something happens, rather than letting it occur as God instructs, in his time. Are there any rocks that you need to stop poking? Remember short-term, the results may still look good, and make you feel better for a moment, but in the long-term you may not reach the promised land that God has for you.

Make a list of the times when you know you have 'poked the rock', and those areas where you know you may be prone to do it again. Confess these things to God and a close friend.

Today's action is actually a resolution to inactivity rather than activity, when we need to let go, and let God. Pray for wisdom to know these moments.

NOTES ●◆

120

WORM-CATCHING

Genesis 27

Get up before any of your neighbours would be up, and walk through your neighbourhood. Pray for the families you know and those you don't know, working your way strategically around an area. Pray for the days that they are about to wake up to. Pray that today will be different for them, right from the moment they wake, because you have prayed God's blessing on them. Recently I've been reading the stories of Genesis, and my mind has been blown by the power of a spoken blessing. Once a blessing has been spoken, even if it is to the wrong brother (as with Jacob and Esau), it cannot be retracted (v33). This is underlined when Israel is passing on a blessing to Joseph's children in Genesis 48:15-20.

Pray that today a window would open for your neighbours to see something of God at work in his world. If you're struggling for words, it may be good to pray a repeated prayer slowly at each stopping point, such as the one below. However leave space for God to prompt you in certain directions or prayers. There may be a specific family situation or current tension in an area that is beating on God's heart. If you spot someone else doing it, greet them with a suitably secret signal!

Father God. Reveal your love and truth today to those who live in this small corner of your broken world. Heal here Lord. May your blessing rest here. Amen.

NOTES

BIBLIOGRAPHY

1. Mark Miller, Experiential Storytelling (Grand Rapids: Zondervan, 2004)
2. Brian Walsh and Sylvia Keesmat, Colossians Remixed: Subverting the empire (Milton Keynes: Paternoster, 2005)
3. Margaret Mead, Some Personal Views (Walker & co, 1979)
4. Bono and Michka Assayas, Bono on Bono (London: Hodder & Stoughton, 2005)
5. Derek Kidner, The Message of Ecclesiastes, The Bible speaks today series (Leicester: IVP, 1988)
6. Ron Sider, Rich Christians in an Age of Hunger (Leicester: IVP, 1977)
7. Vincent Donovan, Christianity Rediscovered (Maryknoll: Orbis 2003)
8. Ronald Rolheiser, The Shattered Lantern (London: Hodder & Stoughton, 1997)
9. Rob Bell, Velvet Elvis (Grand Rapids: Zondervan, 2005)
10. Carl Honore, In Praise of Slow (London: Orion, 2005)
11. Stephen Lawhead, Merlin (Oxford: Lion Hudson, 1988)